AUSTRIAN FOREIGN POLICY
1908–18

AUSTRIAN FOREIGN POLICY, 1908–18

BY

ALFRED FRANCIS PRIBRAM

Professor of History in the University of Vienna

WITH A FOREWORD BY
G. P. GOOCH

ARCHON BOOKS, 1971

First published 1923 George Allen & Unwin Ltd.
Reprinted 1971 with permission
in an unaltered and unabridged edition

ISBN: 0-208-00997-3
Library of Congress Catalog Card Number: 74–147376
Printed in the United States of America

FOREWORD

IN the summer of 1922 Professor Pribram was
invited to deliver three lectures on the Foreign
Policy of Austria before the University of London.
It was a well-deserved compliment to the most
distinguished of living Austrian historians. His
writings on the reign of the Emperor Leopold I
and his collection of the treaties between his
country and our own have long been familiar to
students ; but it is through *The Secret Treaties
of Austria-Hungary* that his name has become
known to wider circles. When the realm of the
Habsburgs ceased to exist in 1918, he obtained
permission from the Government of the Austrian
Republic to examine and publish the agreements
concluded between 1879, when the Austro-German
Alliance was formed, and the outbreak of the Great
War. No single volume published during the
present century has thrown such a flood of light
on the European system which produced and
perished in the catastrophe of 1914. An American
translation of the work has appeared, and a French
version is in preparation.

The present volume offers a brief but masterly

survey of Austrian diplomacy from the annexation of Bosnia in 1908 to the collapse of the
Central Powers in 1918. In addition to furnish-
ing information based on the Vienna archives, it
enables us to form a clearer vision of the policy
and personality of Aehrenthal and Berchtold,
Czernin and Burian, of the aged Francis Joseph,
the choleric Francis Ferdinand and the luckless
Charles. But the main value of the lectures is
that they narrate the origins and vicissitudes of
the greatest struggle in history, as they are reflected
in the lens of a highly-trained and singularly dis-
passionate mind in Central Europe. If we are
to understand the conflict, we must inquire how
its problems strike observers not only in London
and Rome, Paris and Petrograd, but in Berlin and
Vienna, Budapest, Sofia and Constantinople.   It
is of special importance for us in the West of
Europe to realize the nature of the rivalry between
Austria and Russia, which was the main cause
of the war of 1914.

I commend this little book to the attention
not only of historical students, but of all who take
an intelligent interest in foreign affairs.

G. P. GOOCH.

PREFACE

THE following account of Austrian Foreign Policy
and its directors during the decade 1908–18 co-
incides in part with that contained in the articles
contributed by me in 1921 to the new volumes of
the *Encyclopædia Britannica* (12th edition, 1922).
My grateful acknowledgments are due to the
Editor and Proprietors of that work for permission
to reproduce the substance of them in these pages.
I have, however, taken the opportunity to embody
such corrections and changes as were required
by there not having been time, before the
Encyclopædia articles were printed, for the English
translations of my German originals to be submitted
for my own revision. Thus the present text, in
so far as it may occasionally differ from corresponding passages there, is that which is to be
preferred as more exactly representing the statements for which I assume responsibility.

Not wishing to exceed the limits allotted to
me, I have had to refrain from quoting the
documents and books of which I have made use.
The former were derived without exception from
the Vienna State Archives. The second and third

volumes of Friedjung's *Das Zeitalter des Imperialismus*, which was left unfinished at the author's death in 1920 and revised by myself, contain most valuable material. For the opening remarks on the internal development of the Monarchy—which were for the purpose of introducing an English audience to this extremely complicated problem—I have used, in addition to other authorities, the first section of Josef Redlich's book, *Das Osterreichische Reichs- und Staatsproblem*, published in 1920.

A. F. PRIBRAM.

VIENNA, *February*, 1923.

CONTENTS

9

AUSTRIAN FOREIGN POLICY

CHAPTER I

BEFORE THE WAR

1908–14

THE final chapter of the foreign policy of Austria-Hungary, which ended with the collapse of the old Monarchy, may be regarded from various points of view : the philosophical, the moral, the political, and the purely historical. I have chosen the last, though I am quite aware that it is the least attractive ; I have done so because from this angle alone can I hope to shed new light upon the subject, and because I believe that the period is still too recent to be judged from any higher standpoint. Furthermore, I shall carefully avoid taking any stand with regard to the question of the causes which have led to the great conflict of nations. For in my opinion these causes are too manifold and too deep-rooted to be summed up in common phrases about Austria-Hungary's wish to expand her spheres of influence in the Balkans, Germany's striving for world-power,

Russia's longing for the warm water, the irrepress-
ible desire of France to recover Alsace-Lorraine,
or England's uneasiness about the growth of
Germany's fleet and commerce. To inquire more
deeply into the nature of these causes would
necessitate a detailed account, which will not be
possible until the archives of all the belligerent
nations are made accessible to serious scholars.
That is what I desire with all my heart ; but I
am afraid it will be a very long time till the
example of Austria-Hungary and Germany is
followed by the other belligerent nations. Then,
and only then, will it be possible to determine,
what degree of so-called guilt—I would prefer to
say responsibility—rests on individual peoples, not
to say individual men, for having precipitated the
World War. The task I have set myself is more
restricted. My object is only to present the most
important facts of Austria-Hungary's foreign policy
in the years 1908–18, and their causal connec-
tions, without any political or moral reflections.
I wish to emphasize that this policy was the work
of the Austro-Hungarian Government, not of the
people of that State. For the people had no
decisive active part in foreign policy, either directly
or indirectly through their representatives in
Parliament, where, in fact, a strong party of
prominent members disapproved the policy of the
Government. The foreign policy of Austria-
Hungary was the work of the Sovereign and of

a few men in office. To what degree these men were affected by the attitude of the various nationalities, by party influences, by the traditions of the social class to which they belonged, would be an exceedingly interesting subject for historical research, which I, however, must ignore ; since I fear that even my more restricted treatment of the subject will make very considerable demands upon your attention and patience. But I hope that you will not find it entirely without interest to hear, for the first time, an account—based on the impartial examination of the documents—of events during the last fateful decade of the Austro-Hungarian Monarchy.

That the internal and foreign policies of a State are considerably affected the one by the other is evident to anyone engaged in historical study. This reciprocal influence can be traced with more certainty in the Austro-Hungarian Monarchy than in any other State. In order to understand its foreign policy during the last decade of its existence it is, therefore, necessary briefly to trace its internal development up to the point at which our narrative is to begin. This is the more necessary because events which previously concerned only the fate of the Danubian Monarchy itself later became questions of world import.

It has often been said that the Empire of the Habsburgs was the result of lucky marriages, and that it has always been a sort of " political

monstrosity." This is a mistake. This explana-
tion does not hold, not even as regards the large
non-Austrian territories that fell into the hands of
the Habsburgs in the course of centuries. It
certainly does not hold for the territories of the
Austro-Hungarian Monarchy as it developed into
a Great Power from the sixteenth to the eighteenth
centuries, after the union of the German hereditary
lands with the possessions of the Bohemian
and Hungarian crowns. In fact, geographical,
economical and religious factors played an even
larger part in this process than the conscious
acts of individual rulers and their advisers. These
men left nothing undone in using the power of
the dynastic-absolute State which was at their
disposal to transform the various nationalities of
their Empire into a German Greater Austria ; and
there were times when it seemed as though they
would attain their end. The fact that their plans
did not materialize is due partly to the stubborn
resistance of the various peoples, partly to the
circumstance that the Habsburgs were never in
a position to devote their entire energy to this
great and difficult undertaking. Their position
as Roman Emperors, their international interests
as rulers of countries scattered throughout Europe,
the cultural task of defending Western Christianity
against the menaces of the Turks—all these and
other considerations made it impossible for them
to devote their whole strength to the construction

of a unified State on a German basis.   Whether
or not under other conditions the Habsburgs would
have succeeded in realizing their object in the
course of the seventeenth and eighteenth centuries
is a question which I will not attempt to answer.
But one thing is certain : ever since the nine-
teenth century, ever since the time when the idea
of nationality began to pervade the whole public
life of Europe, when it began greatly to influence
the policies of the Cabinets and became one of
the leading tendencies in modern Europe's international relations, the time for the Germanization
of the Monarchy was past.   The revolution of
1848 made it perfectly clear to the whole world
that there was in Austria an exceedingly difficult
problem to be solved ; that the question would
now have to be decided whether or not this State
could be reconstituted according to modern ideas.

Austria had in 1848 enough men who deemed
it possible to solve the problems of nationality
and unity in accordance with the spirit of the
time, and who worked towards this end ; but
their powers were not sufficient to overcome the
resistance offered by the Crown and its advisers.
The latter still hoped to stop the rolling wheel
of history.   The motto of Francis Joseph, *Viribus
Unitis*, was interpreted to mean " the strength
of all for the interests of the dynasty."   The
Government proceeded as before the revolution,
and hoped to suppress the nationalist movement

by the application of force. But the Austrian
statesmen were doomed to failure, when in the
years 1849–60 they tried to melt down the
heterogeneous parts of the monarchy into a
unitary State under German leadership ; for they
only alienated the various peoples of the Empire.
The South Slavs in particular complained, not
unjustly, of the ingratitude of the dynasty which
they had served so faithfully in suppressing the
rebellious peoples in the year 1848. From that
time dates their estrangement from the Emperor
and the Empire ; through them the plan of 1861,
to give the whole Empire a common legislature,
was wrecked.

The Austrian unified State broke down after
the battle of Sadowa. By the settlement of 1867
the dynasty reached an understanding with the
Magyar nobility, and granted to it an ever-increasing influence, which the latter succeeded in
utilizing to strengthen its position not only in
relation to the Crown and the other half of the
Empire, but also in relation to the non-Magyar
inhabitants of Hungary itself. These plans of
the Magyar aristocracy were furthered by the
confusion which continued within the Austrian
part of the Empire, where Germans and Czechs
stood irreconcilably opposed to each other. All
attempts of the Government to mediate between
the two were in vain. In spite of the most
generous concessions, the Government failed to win

over the Czechs, who increased their national demands from decade to decade ; whereas the Germans, faithful heretofore to the dynasty and the idea of unification, were only offended thereby. So it happened that all the different races gradually deserted the ruling family, and, regardless of the common interests, began to seek only their own advantage. In Hungary, the party whose ultimate object was the dissolution of the bond between the two halves of the Empire gained in influence, and drove the supporters of the settlement of 1867 to make more and more demands on the Crown, demands which Francis Joseph granted in large measure, in so far as they did not impair the unity of the army and the rights of the dynasty. These successes of the Magyars had their marked effect on the other races. In Bohemia the influence of the nationalist circles, which demanded for their country the same rights as had been granted to the Magyars in Hungary, grew from year to year. The Poles, who had for decades been favoured by the Austrian Government, knew exceedingly well how to further their plans, which aimed at the greatest possible autonomy and power over the non-Polish population of the country. The South Slavs, however, who now began to pursue the same object, but did not feel themselves equally supported by the dynasty in their struggle to defend their independence against the Germans, and especially against the increasing aggressiveness of

2

the Magyars, cast more and more longing glances across the border at their brothers in Serbia, and listened to the enticements of those who represented the idea of a Greater Serbia.

The danger threatening the Empire from the attitude of the South Slavs was not unknown to the Governments in Vienna and Budapest. Both were determined to appease it ; but the steps they took for this purpose were different. Most of the Hungarian statesmen advocated the use of force, while the Austrians preferred conciliation. Both methods failed. The danger increased when the rather Russophil Karageorgeovich dynasty ascended the Serbian throne in succession to the Obrenovich, which had inclined towards Austria. Henceforth, Belgrade became the centre of all Pan-Serbian agitation. From there was preached incessantly the struggle against the Danubian Monarchy, whose commanding position in the Balkans was described as the only obstacle to the realization of the nationalist desires of all South Slavs. The words of the Serbian Minister Protich, that peace could be maintained between the Monarchy and the Balkan States only if the former should decide to play the part of an Eastern Switzerland, became a slogan which spread from Belgrade and found more and more recognition and favour in the South Slav territories of the Habsburgs. That this danger would have to be met was generally recognized in the leading circles of Vienna and Budapest ; but the Governments still hesitated whether force should be used, or whether the South Slavs should be reconciled by concessions. Time passed, and nothing was done. The South Slav sore, allowed to fester on the body of the Empire, spread over it until it brought about its death.

The responsibility for this fact, so fateful for the Empire and for the dynasty, rests largely with Francis Joseph, who in the last years of his reign continued to strive to preserve peace for his realm, but avoided decisive measures.

In all questions affecting the constitution of the Monarchy, and in particular the relations between Austria and Hungary, he stood in the later years of his reign by the principles of the settlement of 1867. He would not consider the federation of the Empire, but stood unmoved on the basis of dualism. He went far to meet the efforts of the Hungarian Government for independence, but refused energetically during this period demands tending towards the severing of the remaining bonds between the two halves of the Monarchy, especially that of the united army. In the increasingly violent conflicts between the different nationalities inhabiting the Cis-Leithan territories, he stood above party. This was the easier for him on account of his indifference towards all the nationalities of his vast realm, even towards the Germans, although to the end of his life he felt himself to be a German prince. As in the earlier part of his reign, so in the last decade, the separate nationalities were favoured or neglected, but always played off against one another.

Francis Joseph was not one of those of whom contemporaries, especially those at a distance, form any definite impression. The reserve which he maintained even towards the great majority of his advisers made it more difficult to penetrate into his real nature. He had a deep sense of his exalted position as a ruler. To the end of his days he remained profoundly convinced that the Empire over which he ruled was *his* Empire and the peoples *his* peoples. This conception of the majesty of the office bestowed on him by God found expression in his bearing. He always maintained a regal attitude. He showed kindliness and winning courtesy to everyone. Nothing was farther from him than posing, and no one ever heard him utter high-sounding phrases ; but he avoided every kind of intimacy even in his intercourse with members of the Imperial House and, even with them, knew how to maintain his distance. His intellectual gifts were not remarkable, but he possessed sound common sense and mother wit. He had a strikingly good memory for persons and events. As a ruler he was a model of the sense of duty. From early morning to evening he attended to business with clock-like regularity, and dealt with all the documents laid before him with the greatest punctuality. This industry and his exact memory made him one of the best authorities in all Government affairs. He sometimes startled his ministers by his intimate knowledge of the details of the business in hand, and occasionally embarrassed them. But he went no farther than the details, and lacked the power of surveying the whole. He also lacked, especially in his later years, the ability to take the initiative in important questions, to form independent resolutions and to carry them to their logical conclusion. In an ever-increasing degree he left the decision to his responsible ministers. He was not without skill in the choice of his advisers, but had an instinctive dislike to men whom he felt to be his intellectual superiors. He also disliked people of independent character, and even within the family circle he preferred those who were more sub-servient. He was essentially cold in temperament, with great self-control, increased by practice. Among European rulers he enjoyed great respect during the last decades of his reign, which he owed to his age, his great experience, his personal charm, his blameless conduct, and above all to the fact that his word could be relied upon. He was a faithful son of the Catholic Church and looked up with reverence to the Holy Father ; but, quite in the spirit of the traditions of his House, he preserved the rights of the dynasty and of the State with the utmost tenacity, even against the Pope. He took no interest in the arts and sciences, being in this respect more of a Lorrainer than a Habsburg ; but, whenever he expressed an opinion on these subjects, he showed a decided aversion, to modern tendencies in music, literature and art.

The above-mentioned connection between the internal and external policy becomes clear in recalling the main historical problem of the foreign policy of the old Monarchy. Since the foundation of the German Empire and the kingdom of united Italy, an extension of Austria-Hungary towards the south and west of Europe had become impossible. Only in the south-east could she still count on an expansion of her territory and power. Thus from the 'seventies onwards the policy of the leading Austro-Hungarian statesmen had taken the direction indicated by geographical conditions.

In this direction Austria had to reckon with the opposition of Russia, which, with the pressing back of Turkish influence, had become her great rival in south-eastern Europe. In order to maintain herself as a Great Power, render her frontiers secure against hostile attacks and suffer no restriction on her further development, she could not allow another Great Power to command the Danube and its mouths and arrogate to itself the hegemony of the Balkan peoples. This political and economic opposition between the Habsburg Monarchy and Russia was reinforced by rivalry of a racial and cultural nature. In view of this struggle against a competitor far superior in population and military strength, Austrian statesmen had sought an alliance or understanding with those European States whose interests appeared to run parallel with their own. It was to the benevolent attitude of Germany and England that Austria had owed the occupation of Bosnia and Herzegovina and the right of maintaining garrisons in the Sanjak of Novibazar—the door to the Near East and the first step towards an expansion of Austria-Hungary's sphere of influence in the Balkans, which promised rich prospects, but at the same time an increase in Russian hostility.

From the early 'eighties Andrassy's successors did indeed try to arrive at a *modus vivendi* with Russia, and were zealously seconded in this effort by Prince Bismarck, who wished to hold the balance between his two allies, and, to reach this end, incessantly urged the Viennese Cabinet to conclude an agreement with that of Petrograd in regard to spheres of influence in the Balkans. Numerous crises were overcome ; but the conflict of interest remained, and was intensified after the Russo-Japanese War. Russian statesmen renounced the policy of reaching the " warm water " in the Far East, and returned to that of Peter the Great and Catherine and never entirely given up, the goal of which had been the conquest of Constanti-

nople and the command of the Dardanelles. The
constantly increasing differences between Germany
and the Western Powers, and the advances made
by the latter towards friendship with the court
of the Tsar, led in 1907–8 to a close entente
between Russia and England, and hence to the
development of the long-standing alliance between
Russia and France into a Triple Entente.

From the autumn of 1906 Baron Aehrenthal
directed the foreign policy of the Habsburg
Monarchy. There is no doubt that he was a
statesman of considerable mark, a man of wide
knowledge and well-ordered intelligence. He was
ambitious, but not vain, and an untiring worker.
Moreover, in moments of great excitement he was
able to maintain outward calm. He was convinced of his own value, but had no desire to
parade it.

Even during his lifetime the estimate of his foreign
policy fluctuated violently. On the one hand it
was blamed as provocative, on the other as weak.
After the disastrous result of the World War, bringing with it the downfall of the Habsburg Monarchy,
it is still more difficult to answer the question
whether the path pursued by him was the right
one. It is certain that the Entente Powers were
drawn more closely together by the active part
played, during his period of office, by Austria-
Hungary in Balkan affairs. It is true that the
chances of success for the Central Powers in an

international struggle were better in the years 1909 and 1911 than in 1914. But the question remains undecided whether, if his activity had been longer continued, Aehrenthal would have been able to maintain the position of Austria-Hungary as a Great Power without an appeal to the decision of arms. As early as 1907 he recognized the threatening danger, which became greater and greater as the internal affairs of the Turkish Empire assumed a more and more critical aspect. This Empire he wished to preserve, if it could by any means be done ; but in the event of its final liquidation he was firmly determined to safe-guard the interests of Austria-Hungary. It was above all necessary to make sure of the possession of the occupied provinces of Bosnia and Herze-govina, which had been under Austro-Hungarian government for thirty years past, and for which the Monarchy had done so much in raising the material and cultural condition of the country. Moreover, he considered the annexation as the indispensable preliminary to the building up of the constitution of these provinces, which would give to their inhabitants a limited measure of self-government.

The Young Turk revolution in July, 1908, offered the immediate occasion for carrying into effect the annexation of these territories. It happened opportunely that at this very time Russian statesmen wished to realize their designs

on the Dardanelles. Isvolsky knew, indeed, that
it would not be easy to win over Great Britain
to his plans. But since he believed himself sure
of French support, he hoped to achieve at least
his immediate aim, the opening of the Straits to
Russian warships, as soon as he had come to an
understanding with the Central Powers, and
especially with Austria-Hungary. During the
negotiations entered upon between the Cabinets of
Vienna and Petrograd, he gave his consent to the
annexation of Bosnia and Herzegovina, granted
already by Russia to Austria-Hungary by several
treaties concluded in the 'eighties, in the event of
the Vienna Government falling in with his plans
as to the Straits. Aehrenthal seized upon this
proposal, for he hoped that the annexation of
these provinces would enable him to take active
measures in face of the ever-increasing peril of
the Greater Serbia movement.

At the beginning of July, 1908, Isvolsky
forwarded a memorandum which guaranteed to
the Habsburg Monarchy Bosnia and Herzegovina
and the greater part of the Sanjak of Novibazar.
Aehrenthal accepted Isvolsky's offer in so far as
it applied to the annexation of Bosnia and
Herzegovina ; but he demanded the same right
for the warships of Rumania and Bulgaria as for
those of Russia, and in addition a guarantee against
an attack on Constantinople by a Russian fleet
entering the Bosporus. In return he was ready

to give up the Sanjak and the rights appertaining to Austria-Hungary in Montenegro, and therewith the plan of an advance on Salonika, the seizure of which Andrassy had had in view as the next objective in Austria-Hungary's policy of expansion in south-east Europe. After having secured in principle the consent of Germany and Italy, Aehrenthal met Isvolsky on September 15 at the château of Buchlau in Moravia, informed him of the impending Austrian annexation of Bosnia and Herzegovina, and promised him in return a free hand in his proceedings with regard to the question of the Dardanelles. The ministers promised each other mutual support, Aehrenthal renouncing the Sanjak of Novibazar, and Isvolsky promising that Russia would not take possession of Constantinople. A European conference was to give its sanction to their settlement. A binding written agreement was contemplated, but was not arrived at on this occasion.

When, however, at the beginning of October, 1908, Francis Joseph publicly announced the annexation of Bosnia and Herzegovina as a *fait accompli*, a storm of indignation burst forth in many quarters. It was insisted, especially in England, that agreements settled by international treaties could only be modified with the consent of all the contracting Powers. Both in Paris and in London, where Isvolsky had betaken himself in order to obtain the approval of the Western

Powers to the measures which he had concerted with Aehrenthal, he met with a decided refusal. Disappointed in his expectations, he now declared that he had been led astray by Aehrenthal, and launched a bitter campaign against him. The differences concerned chiefly two points. Isvolsky maintained that he had referred at Buchlau to the unlawfulness of the plans of Aehrenthal and only promised him not to oppose the annexation of Bosnia and Herzegovina, while Aehrenthal wrote immediately after the conversation to Francis Joseph that the Russian Minister had promised a benevolent attitude in case Austria should proceed to the annexation of these two provinces. Count Berchtold, to whom both statesmen had given a report of this conversation immediately after it had taken place, confirmed on his word of honour the assertions of Aehrenthal. Secondly, Isvolsky denied that a date had been fixed for the annexa-tion, while Aehrenthal asserted that he had explained that it might be necessary to carry out the annexation at the beginning of October, though he had promised to inform him beforehand—as he did—of the exact date.

Encouraged by the attitude of the Great Powers, especially of England and Russia, Serbia lodged a protest against the annexation, demanded autonomy for the territories under the guarantee of the Great Powers, and a port on the Adriatic, with a strip of territory to connect it with Serbia. Since

Austria-Hungary showed no inclination to take these demands into consideration, Serbia now began to strengthen her military forces. At the same time a violent anti-Austrian movement began to make itself felt in Turkey. All goods coming from Austria-Hungary were boycotted, and Austro-Hungarian traders living in Turkey were subjected to annoyance. Bulgaria, whose Prince had assumed the royal title on October 5, 1908, also took sides against Austria-Hungary, and entered into negotiations with Russia and Serbia. In Italy, too, a hostile tendency towards Austria had gained the upper hand. Victor Emmanuel described the annexation of Bosnia and Herzegovina as a stab at the Treaty of Berlin, and Tittoni, who had spoken on October 7 in terms favourable to the annexation, declared in the Italian Chamber at the beginning of December—despite a letter which he had addressed to Aehrenthal on October 4 and negotiations which led on October 8 to an agreement—that he had entered into no engagements with regard to it. The Nationalist Press and the Irredentists fanned the flames, and in the Austrian Parliament the Slavs, and above all Kramarz, the Czech leader, who at first, on advice from Petrograd, had consented to the annexation, now raised loud complaints against the proceedings of the Government.

Aehrenthal remained firm. He was convinced that Russia, who had not yet recovered from the

Russo-Japanese War, would not draw the sword, and that he would therefore succeed in achieving his ends without bloodshed. His own efforts were directed towards the preservation of peace. In this point of view he was at odds with a powerful party, led by Conrad von Hötzendorf, chief of the Austro-Hungarian General Staff, which was in favour of a decision by force of arms. In order to meet Russia's views, Aehrenthal consented to the convening of a European conference, but insisted that he could only promise Serbia and Montenegro economic compensation, and made it a condition that the question of Austria-Hungary's sovereignty over Bosnia and Herzegovina should not be discussed. His attitude aroused violent indignation in London and Paris. But since Germany resolutely took her stand on the side of the Habsburg Monarchy, and France, with an eye to her Moroccan interests, only gave a lukewarm support to the Russian demands, Isvolsky found himself compelled to beat a retreat. As early as December, 1908, he agreed that the conference should recognize the annexation of Bosnia and Herzegovina, after a previous discussion of the matter had taken place between the several Cabinets.

Meanwhile, the greatest difficulties were caused to Aehrenthal by the attitude of the British Cabinet, which did not want war, but desired the diplomatic defeat of Austria. Sir Edward Grey worked in this sense in Serbia and Turkey. He advised the Turkish Government to allow their consent to the annexation of Bosnia and Herzegovina to be bought by a proportionate cash indemnity. Aehrenthal fell in with this suggestion and on February 26, 1909, concluded an agreement with Turkey, which secured to the Sultan, in return for his recognition of the annexation of Bosnia and Herzegovina, £2,500,000 in compensation for Ottoman State property in the annexed provinces. In March the negotiations as to the form of consent to the annexation to be given by the Great Powers concerned were brought to a conclusion. It was to be effected by official declarations on their part, a European conference being thus avoided.

On March 24 declarations in this sense were handed in at Berlin and Vienna by the Russian Government ; those of England followed on March 28.

Meanwhile, the danger of an Austro-Serbian war, which for some time had appeared inevitable, had fortunately passed by. Even after the settlement of the Austro-Turkish conflict the Serbs remained stubborn ; but Aehrenthal wanted to avoid war, and now, as before, hoped to attain his end by calm firmness and conciliation. At the beginning of March he declared that Serbia, in order to avoid the humiliation of having her fate settled by the statesmen of Vienna, might submit to the decision of the Great Powers. But the Serbian Government declined, and continued to arm. The Cabinet of Vienna then decreed that the troops in the south-east of the Monarchy should be reinforced. Isvolsky now saw that Francis Joseph was in earnest. Since he could not venture on war, he accepted the proposal of the German Chancellor, Bülow, that Russia herself should use her influence over Serbia in the direction of moderation. On Great Britain's initiative, negotiations were entered upon with the Government of Vienna, which led to the drafting of a note which should secure to Austria-Hungary the satisfaction which she demanded. After overcoming great difficulties an agreement was reached. On March 31 the Serbian Government presented a note at Vienna in which it declared that Serbia had not suffered any injury to her rights through the annexation of Bosnia and Herzegovina, and promised to change the attitude which she had hitherto taken up towards the Habsburg Monarchy, to maintain good neighbourly relations with Austria-Hungary, and to reduce her army to the footing of the previous year. In so doing Serbia submitted to the behest of the Signatory Powers, but at the same time to the will of Austria-Hungary. Montenegro thereupon followed suit. The event was a victory for Aehrenthal, but a Pyrrhic victory, since it intensified the cleavage of Europe into two hostile camps. Russia now broke definitely with Austria-Hungary and became increasingly hostile to German policy, while England recognized ever more clearly the significance of the Southern Slavs in the struggle against Germany, and especially of Serbia as a battering-ram against Germany's ally, the Habsburg Monarchy.

Two other events led to a further strengthening of the Triple Entente. One was the *rapprochement* between Russia and Italy, made manifest by the Tsar's visit to Racconigi (October 24, 1909). The other was the secret treaty concluded in December, 1909, between Russia and Bulgaria, which ranged the latter in the Russian sphere of influence, and contained, among other things, the declaration that the realization of the ideals of the Slav peoples in the Balkan Peninsula would only be possible after a Russian victory over Germany and Austria-Hungary—the first open confession that the Russian Government anticipated a war with the Central Powers as inevitable.

Yet at this time these opposing tendencies did not come out into the open. The Central Powers sought rather to overcome them. At the beginning of 1910 negotiations took place with Russia to restore friendly relations, but after hopeful preliminaries they split on the irreconcilability of conflicting interests. Aehrenthal's efforts at Rome seemed more promising. At the end of 1909 he reached an agreement on the Albanian question by which further friction between the two States,

who were rivals in this quarter, should be avoided.
In subsequent conversations in 1910 with the
Italian Foreign Minister, San Giuliano, measures
were considered which should smooth the way
towards the establishment of friendly relations
between the Cabinets of Vienna and Rome.   In
1910 and 1911, moreover, Aehrenthal was eagerly
striving for the maintenance of peace.   He
endeavoured to reconcile the differences which were
for ever cropping up anew between England and
Germany. In the Moroccan question, it is true, he
ranged himself on the side of his ally, but he took
pains to abstain from irritating the other side.   In
order to win over Rumania and conciliate Serbia,
commercial treaties were concluded with them.   In
the interest of peace, too, he placed no obstacle
in the way of the assumption of the royal title by
the Prince of Montenegro (August 29, 1910).

Yet Aehrenthal kept his aim steadfastly in view,
namely, the upholding of Austria-Hungary's interests
in the Near East ; and he left the Balkan peoples
in no doubt that he would not be a passive
spectator of the downfall of Turkey.   He was
in a difficult position when, in the autumn of 1911,
Italy seized the opportunity for taking possession
of Tripoli.   A strong party, headed by the Chief
of the General Staff, Conrad von Hötzendorf,
held that the moment had arrived for a reckoning
with their faithless ally.   In any case they wanted
to use this favourable opportunity for assuring to

Austria-Hungary the hegemony of the Balkans. But Aehrenthal stood for the maintenance of the Triple Alliance. He declared in a memorandum to the Emperor that the tradition of the Habsburg policy forbade the breach of treaties. He even held that it was in the interest of the Monarchy that Italy's Imperialist aspirations should find satisfaction on the south of the Mediterranean. He therefore requested Italy, while leaving her a free hand in Tripoli, not to interfere with the designs of the Vienna Cabinet in the Balkan Peninsula. In this connection he requested the withdrawal of the Italian fleet from the coast of Albania, and protested against Italian designs on Salonika.

The fact that Aehrenthal gained his ends by these demands confirmed him in the idea that he had hit upon the right path, and increased his hopes of being able to guard Austria-Hungary's interests in this difficult crisis without resorting to arms. His death (February 17, 1912) was therefore a heavy loss to the Monarchy, which made itself all the more felt since just at that time new dangers were arising for it in South-East Europe.

The Italo-Turkish War, and especially the closing of the Dardanelles at the instance of the Turks, had severely damaged Russian trade, and increased the desire of Russian statesmen to gain command of the Black Sea. It was also widely held that this was a favourable opportunity to bring about a Balkan Alliance under Russian leadership, which should make it possible for Russia, as protector of the Slav peoples of the Balkans, to take possession of Constantinople.   Hartwig, the Russian Minister in Belgrade, was particularly active in this direction.   Other circles, led by Tcharykov, the Russian Ambassador in Constantinople, thought it possible to attain the same end by other means.   They wanted to preserve Turkey, but to make her Russia's vassal.   She was to be admitted to the Balkan Alliance and, in return, to allow the Russian fleet a free exit to the Mediterranean.   But Tcharykov's efforts failed.   Turkey refused, and in March, 1912, he had to leave Constantinople.

The old plan of forming a Balkan Alliance against Turkey was now taken up again.   The greatest difficulty in its way was the jealousy between the Bulgarians, on the one hand, and the Serbs and Greeks on the other.   Bulgaria would not hear of conceding to these peoples the extensions of territory which they claimed in Macedonia. It was not till March, 1912, when the Russophil Gueshoff Cabinet came into power in Sofia, that the Serbo-Bulgarian treaty was concluded, which was indeed aimed in the first place against Turkey, but also had the Habsburg Monarchy in view. Two military conventions (of May 12 and July 12, 1912) further developed the Serbo-Bulgarian Alliance.   Bulgaria now undertook, in case Austria-Hungary occupied the Sanjak of Novibazar, to contribute 200,000 men towards a war with this

Power.   On May 29 Ferdinand of Bulgaria concluded a treaty with Greece against Turkey.   But
at the same time he handed in peaceful declarations at Vienna, Berlin and Constantinople, and let
himself be fêted in Vienna as a friend of the
Habsburg Monarchy.   At the beginning of July,
1912, the Tsar, at his meeting with the German
Emperor at Baltisch Port in Esthonia, laid stress
upon his pacific intentions.   But as early as August
began the long-prepared conflict of the Christian
peoples of the Balkans with Turkey, leading to
bloody local struggles, in which there was no lack
of atrocities on either side.

In vain did the Central Powers endeavour to
bring about an intervention of the Great Powers
of Europe.   On September 30, 1912, the order
for mobilization was issued in Sofia, Belgrade and
Athens.   Turkey thereupon determined to end the
war against Italy by sacrificing Tripoli and the
Cyrenaica ; and on October 18, 1912, the treaty
of peace was signed at Lausanne.   Meanwhile the
Balkan States had completed the last preparations
for war.   On October 8 Montenegro declared war
on Turkey, and on October 17 and 18 Serbia,
Bulgaria and Greece followed suit.   To the aston-
ishment of the Great Powers, which, in expectation
of a Turkish victory, had declared that the *status
quo* should not be altered whatever might happen
in the course of the war, the Christian States gained
decisive victories from the outset.   The battle of

Kirkilisse (October 22) went in favour of the Bulgars, that of Kumanovo (October 26) in favour of the Serbs.   The Turkish troops, falling back rapidly, did indeed defend themselves successfully on the Chatalja lines against the oncoming Bulgarians, and thereby saved their threatened capital. But since none of the Great Powers would take active measures in favour of the Turks, they could not hope to reconquer the lost provinces.   On December 3 an armistice was concluded between Turkey and Serbia and between Turkey and Bulgaria. Greece took no part in it, but continued the struggle.

The success of the Balkan States against Turkey weakened the prestige of Austria-Hungary in the Balkans.   The entry of the Greeks into Salonika (November 8, 1912), and the advance of the Serbian troops to the Adriatic, produced a particularly painful impression in Vienna.   But consideration for the Slav peoples of the Monarchy, who hailed with joy the victory of the Christian States of the Balkans over Turkey, and the dread of incurring the open enmity of Russia by an energetic intervention on behalf of the Sultan, held the Vienna Government back, and disposed it, as early as the end of October, 1912, to modify its demands.   Albania was to be allowed to develop freely ; Serbian aspirations towards the Adriatic were to be rejected, and Rumania's claims to an extension of territory to be considered.   Count Berchtold, who, after having repeatedly urged that he considered himself unfit for the post, succeeded Aehrenthal in February, 1912, demanded no more than security for economic interests in the Balkans.

On this account he refused in the most decided terms to consent to the proposal of the French Government that Austria-Hungary, like all the other Great Powers, should express her *désinteressement* in the events taking place.

In so far as his plans concerned Albania and Serbia, Berchtold found Italian politicians in favour of them, since they saw in the spread of the Slav peoples to the Adriatic a danger to Italy, to oppose which in good time seemed to them more important than any further check to the influence of the Habsburg Monarchy, divided as it was against itself.   The common danger brought about a *rapprochement* between the two Cabinets, which was strengthened by Italy's annoyance at the attitude of France at the time of the Tripoli war. Thus it happened that, as far back as December 5, 1912, in spite of violent opposition on the part of the nationalist deputies, of the more important section of the Press, and of Italian public opinion, the Triple Alliance was renewed for another six to twelve years, reckoned from 1914 onwards.

But the moderation displayed by Austria-Hungary in her Balkan policy did not produce the effect which had been hoped for at the Ballplatz.   It weakened her credit in the Balkans, disappointed the few partisans she had there, and encouraged the hopes of her many opponents. Paying no attention to Berchtold's declarations, the Serbs continued their efforts to extend their power to the Adriatic.

On November 10, 1912, Serbian troops reached Alessio. At the same time Serbian politicians laboured to incite the other Balkan peoples against Austria-Hungary, since it was only at her expense that they could hope to find a compensation for the concessions which they had made in the March treaty with Bulgaria. In Petrograd they left no stone unturned to create a strong feeling against Austria-Hungary. In November, 1912, the Russian Cabinet, which had secretly pledged itself to foster the political aspirations of the Serbs, declared itself in favour of the cession of an Adriatic port to Serbia, and was supported in this by France and England. The Russian trial mobilization increased the danger of a collision. The Vienna Government, on its side, proceeded to prepare for war. The fact that Conrad von Hötzendorf was again entrusted with the position of Chief of the General Staff, which he had had to give up a year before because he had spoken in favour of an active military policy, showed that the war party had increased its influence at the Court of Vienna. But the disinclination of the three Emperors to conjure up a world war for the sake of Albania or Serbia, together with the influence of Great Britain, proved stronger than the war parties in either

Vienna or Petrograd. In opposition to Austria-Hungary, Bethmann-Hollweg, the German Chancellor, and Kiderlen-Wächter, the German Foreign Minister, energetically upheld the point of view that a compromise with Russia was both desirable and possible ; and in a like sense William II., when the Archduke Francis Ferdinand tried to convince him at Springe (November 23, 1912) of the necessity of energetic action against the unreasonable demands of the Serbs, insisted that, while he was in favour of using firm language, he was anxious to avoid all steps which might lead to a rupture with Russia. In order that no doubt should arise in the world as to the peace-loving policy of the German Empire, Bethmann-Hollweg, in announcing in the Reichstag (at the beginning of December, 1912) the renewal of the Triple Alliance, added that Germany must leave it to her Austrian ally to realize her aspirations alone, and would only join in a conflict in the case of a war of aggression against her, for the preservation of her own position in Europe and the defence of her own future and security.

Under the impression of these declarations, Berchtold at the end of 1912 rejected Conrad's propositions, which aimed at the occupation of the Sanjak of Novibazar and ridding Albania of Serbian troops, and he sought rather to serve the interests of the Monarchy by diplomacy. In this connection it stood him in good stead that a change had meanwhile come over affairs at the Court of Petrograd, not uninfluenced by external factors, and especially by England. The peace party had gained the upper hand. As late as November, 1912, the Russian Government made a communication at Belgrade to the effect that it would offer no active opposition to the formation of an autonomous Albania, and requesting an attitude of reserve towards Austria-Hungary. Shortly afterwards, on the suggestion of Sir Edward Grey, a conference of Ambassadors in London was decided upon, to take place at the same time as the peace negotiations which were being carried on there between Turkey and her opponents, with a view to finding a solution of the outstanding questions at issue between Russia and Austria-Hungary. After long hesitation, Berchtold, under pressure from Germany and Italy, consented to the conference, but insisted that as a matter of principle Austria-Hungary should take no part in any discussion of the question as to whether Serbia should be permanently established on the Adriatic. Serbia thereupon declared her willingness to yield to the decision of the Great Powers.

Yet the Austro-Hungarian and Russian troops remained under arms, and Serbian intrigues continued. The negotiations of the London conference proceeded slowly. When the peace conference, which was sitting at the same time, came temporarily to an end on January 7, 1913,

owing to Turkey's refusal of the demand that she
should cede the fortresses of Adrianople, Scutari
and Janina, which had not yet fallen, the conference
presided over by Sir Edward Grey made efforts
to prevent a resumption of hostilities.   But these
attempts were unsuccessful.   On February 3, 1913,
began the second Balkan War.   Meanwhile the
deliberations dragged on in London as to the
frontier of the new Albanian State.   Russia in
this matter represented the views of Serbia and
Montenegro, but met with resolute opposition not
only from Austria-Hungary but from Italy.   It
seemed as if it would come to an armed conflict
between Austro-Hungary and Russia ; but at the
last moment the danger was averted.   Prince
Gottfried Hohenlohe was sent on a special mission
to Petrograd, and succeeded in convincing
Nicholas II. of Francis Joseph's pacific intentions.
The negotiations now opened led in March to the
cancelling of the mobilization on the frontiers which
had been set on foot by both Powers.   At the
same time the Russian representative at the London
conference announced his sovereign's readiness to
consent to the allotment of Scutari to Albania, in
the event of Austria-Hungary's acceding to the separation of Djakova, Ipek and Prisren from Albania.
On March 20 the representative of Austria-Hungary
handed in a declaration in the same sense.

By now the war between the Balkan States and
Turkey had taken its course, leading, in spite of

the unexpectedly gallant defence of the Turks, to the fall of Janina (March 6) and Adrianople (March 26).   On account of the wrangling which broke out between Bulgaria on the one hand, and Serbia and Greece on the other, as to the partition of Macedonia, Bulgaria concluded an armistice with Turkey on April 16.   But there was no sign of the peace which was desired on all hands.   Serbia, in defiance of the protest of the Vienna Cabinet, continued to occupy Northern Albania, with Durazzo, and Montenegro continued to besiege Scutari, although the London conference of Ambassadors had assigned it to the Albanian State ; and the Great Powers decided on a naval demonstration against Montenegro, which was not intended seriously by all the participants.   The war party at Vienna, led by Conrad, wished to force the Montenegrins to raise the siege, if necessary by arms, but did not win their point.   On April 23 Scutari fell into the hands of the Montenegrins. It was not till now that Berchtold nerved himself to the declaration that the Habsburg Monarchy would not tolerate such an insult, and made the necessary preparations for armed intervention. Montenegro thereupon submitted to the dictates of the Great Powers.   On May 5 the Montenegrin troops evacuated Scutari, and on the next day the Serbs left Durazzo.   At the end of May peace preliminaries were concluded between the Turks and their opponents.   But it was impossible to arrive at an agreement between the victors as to the division of the territory which had fallen to them.

Notwithstanding the fact that it had had its way so far as Albania was concerned, the prestige of Vienna in the Balkans had seriously diminished in the course of the two wars, not only in the eyes of the victorious peoples, whose self-confidence had mightily increased, but also in the eyes of its Balkan ally, Rumania.   King Charles had wanted to join in from the beginning of the first Balkan War, in order to prevent a hegemony of Bulgaria in the Balkans, and had only allowed himself to be persuaded to renew for the fifth time his alliance with the Powers of the Triple Alliance by an engagement from the Central Powers that they would see that Rumania received a corresponding extension of territory in the south-east.   Silistria and the surrounding territory was what he had in view.   He now strongly pressed the Court of Vienna for the fulfilment of this engagement. Berchtold did, in fact, make every effort to decide the Bulgarian Government in favour of suitable concessions to Rumania.   But when his efforts broke down, those circles in Bucharest which favoured the Triple Entente persuaded King Charles to invoke Russia's mediation in order to acquire the desired increase of territory.   But Russia's success at Sofia did not satisfy the Rumanians, and induced them to join hands with Ferdinand of Bulgaria's enemies.   This was an advantage for Austria-Hungary, which was, however, set off by the increasing influence of the Entente Powers in Rumania.

Austria-Hungary's leading statesmen met with no better success in their efforts to establish permanently friendly relations with Italy. San Giuliano's desire for common action with the Habsburg Monarchy in the Adriatic question had indeed led recently to a *rapprochement* between the two Cabinets. In the course of 1913 German statesmen had also succeeded in persuading Italy to further military commitments and to the conclusion of a naval convention, the object of which was defined as " the attainment of naval supremacy in the Mediterranean by the defeat of the enemy fleets " in a war against the Western Powers—an agreement which will sound incredible to a present-day audience, but which is nevertheless an established fact. But the voice of the Italian Press and of nationalist circles, who demanded more and more insistently the dissolution of the Triple Alliance and union with the Triple Entente, did not leave the Central Powers any confidence in Italy's loyalty to her engagements. Meanwhile, in July, 1913, the third Balkan War had broken out. Serbia and Greece, joined by Rumania and Turkey, advanced against Bulgaria. The latter, left in the lurch by Russia and only supported diplomatically by Austria-Hungary, succumbed, and signed the Peace of Bucharest (August 10, 1913).

The outcome of these three wars meant for the Austro-Hungarian Monarchy a notable loss of prestige in the Balkan Peninsula. Her adversaries in this quarter, Serbia and Montenegro, and especially the former, had achieved a considerable extension of their possessions, and henceforth, being no longer separated by the Sanjak of Novibazar, were in a position to join forces against the Habsburg Monarchy when the right moment came. The Bulgarians, however, disappointed in their hopes, ascribed the humiliating defeat which they had suffered in the third Balkan War to the feeble attitude of the Vienna Cabinet, which had indeed taken the first steps in the direction of active participation in favour of Bulgaria, but had then, out of fear of Russia and under German and Italian pressure, contented itself with a fruitless diplomatic intervention. The fact that Berchtold's efforts to obtain a revision of the Peace of Bucharest in favour of Bulgaria met with no result could not contribute towards strengthening Austria-Hungary's credit at Sofia. On the other hand, the line of action of the Vienna Government, which in its own interest was working incessantly for a compromise between Bulgaria and Rumania, but could satisfy neither of these two Powers, led to a clearly perceptible estrangement between the Courts of Vienna and Bucharest, which enabled the Rumanian friends of the Triple Entente to win from the King his acquiescence in paving the way to better relations with the Western Powers and Russia. The only advantage which balanced these heavy losses of power and prestige for Austria-Hungary was the dissolution of the Balkan League, the revival of which was prevented by the inextinguishable hatred between Serbs and Bulgarians—a fact of all the greater importance for the Vienna Government as its relations with Serbia became more and more strained and the probability of an armed conflict increased.

The London conference of Ambassadors had on July 29, 1913, come to an agreement as to a fundamental law for Albania, and at its final sitting on August 11 had settled its southern frontier, long a subject of controversy. Serbia alone declined to give up the Albanian territories which she had already occupied in defiance of the London decrees, and stood firm in her resistance when the Vienna Government pressed for their evacuation. The growing differences between the Triple Alliance and the Triple Entente meant that no united action could be expected from the European Great Powers. Italy and Germany—the latter more on grounds of prestige, the former because her interests in this case ran parallel with those of Austria-Hungary—associated themselves with the Vienna Government when, on October 15, 1913, it again insisted at Belgrade on the execution of the London decrees. Serbia at first again refused to obey this demand of the Triple Alliance, and stressed the fact that she was willing to act only according to such advice as might be communicated to her by the Triple Entente ; but when, just as he had done in the spring, Berchtold showed that he was in earnest, and on October 19 demanded at Belgrade the evacuation of the Albanian territory occupied by Serbia under threat of force, the Serbians submitted to the dictates of Vienna (October 20) in accordance with advice from the Triple Entente. The Serbian Press, however, continued to create prejudice against the policy of the Ballplatz ; and the Serbian Government used every opportunity of encouraging movements which had as their object the winning over of the Southern Slavs living under the government of the Habsburg Monarchy to the idea of a Greater Serbia.

In Rumania, too, the agitation against Austria-Hungary was making headway every month. The agitation in Bucharest in favour of the Hungarian Rumanians became more and more active, and their liberation from the domination of the Magyars was indicated as a desirable and possible object of Rumanian policy. In order to achieve it, a *rapprochement* was advocated between Rumania and Russia, and a suitable pretext was found in Nicholas II.'s very cordially expressed congratulations on King Charles's successes in the last Balkan War. It is true that the visit of the Rumanian heir to Petrograd (March 27, 1914) did not bring about that open passing over of Rumania into the camp of the Triple Entente which

Russia had hoped for. King Charles could not be brought to this point, and the Rumanian Government, too, did not at that moment want to break definitely with the Central Powers. But the speeches accompanying the exchange of toasts at the meeting of Nicholas II. with Charles at Constanza on June 14, 1914, left no possible doubt that the friends of the Triple Entente had gained the upper hand at Bucharest. As early as this, Count Ottokar Czernin, the representative of Austria-Hungary at Bucharest, expressed the decided opinion that, in the event of a war between the Central Powers and the Triple Entente, King Charles would not fulfil his pledges. At the same time he uttered a warning against under-rating the danger of an encirclement of the Dual Monarchy through the formation of a new Balkan League under the patronage of Russia and France.

To hinder this encirclement became the principal endeavour of Viennese statesmen, who were un-tiringly at work trying to compose the outstanding differences between Bulgaria on the one hand and Turkey and Rumania on the other, and, if possible, also to win over Greece to a closer adhesion to the Central Powers. But all their efforts broke down owing to the divergent interests and the mutual distrust of the Balkan States, which were revealed during the negotiations conducted under the media-tion of the Central Powers during the winter of 1913-14. The Turco-Bulgarian Treaty, which was nearly concluded in May, 1914, did not come to anything, still less did the compromise between Rumania and Bulgaria, which had been furthered with such especial zeal on the part of Vienna. And the *rapprochement* of Greece with the Triple Alliance, desired by the Emperor William, could not be realized, since the claims of the Greeks met with insuperable opposition both in Sofia and in Constantinople.

Not the least of the factors contributing to these unsatisfactory results was the difference of opinion in influential circles in Vienna and Berlin as to the value of the various Balkan States in case of an international conflict. The Emperor William was a resolute opponent of King Ferdinand of Bulgaria, whom he did not trust ; on the other hand, he was firmly convinced that, in case of war, Charles of Rumania would be true to his engagements as an ally. On this account he endeavoured to persuade the Vienna Government to bring Rumania over entirely into the camp of the Triple Alliance, even at the cost of sacrifices and of the danger that Bulgaria might join the opponents of the Central Powers. But Berchtold was afraid that the Bulgarians, left in the lurch by Austria-Hungary, might come to terms with Serbia, Greece and Rumania, and in company with them and with Russia fall upon the Habsburg Monarchy. Hence he held fast to his policy, which saw in the maintenance and exacerbation of the differences

existing between Bulgaria and the other Balkan
States the only means of preventing the formation
of an alliance of all the Balkan peoples against the
Monarchy.   The conflicting points of view of leading statesmen in Vienna and Berlin led to very
lively debates, and threatened seriously to impair
the good understanding between the two Governments.   However, Berchtold gradually succeeded
in bringing round the Emperor William and the
German statesmen to his views.   From March,
1914, onwards it was determined that the union of
Bulgaria with the Central Powers must remain the
main object of their policy, and that agreements
with the rest of the Balkan States must only be
entered into in so far as they should not be in
conflict with the just desires of Bulgaria.

The removal of this discord was hailed with all
the more joy by the Vienna Cabinet since its
relations with Italy were getting more and more
strained.   San Giuliano, it is true, maintained a
correct demeanour towards the Vienna Government,
and worked for a compromise in the ever-recurring
conflicts to which the divergent interests of the two
States in the Balkans gave rise.   It was even
possible, in the discussions which took place
between him and Berchtold at Abbazia in April,
1914, to arrive at an agreement in the Balkan
question, based upon the maintenance of the autonomy of the Albanian State, for the Government
of which Prince William of Wied had been desig-

nated. But the attitude of the Press, influenced by the Triple Entente, and of the deputies with nationalist sympathies, not to speak of the proceedings of the Italian representatives in Albania, made it apparent that influential circles beyond the Alps were endeavouring to frustrate San Giuliano's policy.

In the eyes of leading Viennese statesmen, the sympathy for the Triple Entente, which was displayed by the Italians with ever-increasing frankness, was all the more ominous since they saw that France, Russia and England were taking steps to increase their own military strength, and also had information of the negotiations which were being conducted by all three Governments with those of Spain, Italy and the Balkan States, which were believed to have as their object the isolation of the Central Powers. At that time, however, the outbreak of a world war was not held to be imminent in Vienna, for it was known that negotiations were going on between Berlin and London, aiming at the establishment of better relations. Count Mensdorff, the Austro-Hungarian Ambassador at the Court of St. James's, did his utmost to assist these efforts. But conditions in the Balkans pressed for a decision. In Vienna it was believed that France and Russia had been successful in their efforts to bring into existence a Balkan League which should also include Turkey, and which would have threatened the existence of the Monarchy.

On June 22, 1914, before the assassination of
the heir to the throne of Austria-Hungary, Conrad
von Hötzendorf drew up a memorandum in which
he described the existing conditions in the Balkans
as intolerable, and insisted on the necessity for
using plain language at Bucharest. The Rumanian
Government must be forced, it said, to declare
openly whether it would make common cause with
the Central Powers or not. In the latter case an
attempt must be made to induce Bulgaria, by far-
reaching promises, to bring to a conclusion the
negotiations for an alliance which had been going
on for a considerable time. These views of
Conrad were shared not only in military circles
but also by Austrian statesmen of authority.   In
a memorandum intended for the German Government, which was also drawn up before the murder
of Francis Ferdinand, Count Berchtold [1] emphasized
the urgency of making every effort to form a
Balkan League under the leadership of the Central
Powers, which should include Bulgaria, Rumania,
Greece and Turkey, and have for its objective the
suppression of Serbia as a political power in the
Balkans.

[1] The basis of this document is to be found in a *mémoire*
drawn up by the Envoy Extraordinary and Minister Pleni-
potentiary, Baron Ludwig Flotow. It was later amplified by
Rudolf Pogatscher, who occupied the same position and was
particularly well informed as to the Balkan question. From
the middle of June onwards it was revised by Baron Franz
Matschenko, of the Austro-Hungarian Foreign Office, and
finally by Berchtold.

Before this document was dispatched to Berlin, the news arrived in Vienna that Francis Ferdinand with his consort had been murdered in Sarajevo. With his tragic end began a new period of Austria-Hungary's history, a period which led to the World War and to the downfall of the Dual Monarchy and of the dynasty Habsburg-Lorraine.

Francis Ferdinand, the son of the Archduke Charles Louis, second of the younger brothers of Francis Joseph, received the education usually given to members of the Imperial family—not a very thorough one, as his succession to the throne was not anticipated. In later years, when he had become heir to the throne, he worked with iron industry to fill up the gaps in his education, learning the languages of the nations over whom he appeared to be called to rule, and taking pleasure in obtaining instruction from leading men of science in their special branches of knowledge. Until the death of the Crown Prince Rudolph in 1889—beyond doubt by his own hand—Francis Ferdinand was only known in limited circles, and even then did not at first play any prominent part. For his uncle for a long time gave him no share in the business of government, and only gradually allowed him to exercise greater influence, first in military matters and afterwards occasionally in questions of domestic and foreign politics. Yet until Francis Ferdinand's death the Emperor reserved for himself the final decision in every

question which arose. The difference of outlook of
the two men became more and more marked; for
with advancing age Francis Joseph was less and
less willing to consider far-reaching reforms, was
anxious to avoid any conflict with the nationalities,
and preferred advisers who knew how to untie a
knot instead of cutting it. It is therefore not
surprising that he did not like Francis Ferdinand,
who advised rapid and energetic action, and, if
necessary, methods of violence. So it happened
that the nephew did not take into sufficient consideration the jealousy with which his aged uncle
guarded his rights as a ruler. He repeatedly
spoke of the responsibility which God had
imposed on him with his right of succession ;
he would express curt opinions on men and
things when he knew that they did not
correspond with his uncle's views.

The estrangement increased ; personal contact
became rarer ; Francis Ferdinand came into the
Emperor's presence only on exceptional occasions.
As a rule he contented himself with expressing his
views in writing, and they very rarely agreed with
those of his uncle. For he was decidedly opposed
to the preponderant influence exercised in ever-
increasing measure by the Magyars in both
domestic and foreign affairs, and blamed the com-
plaisance shown by Francis Joseph to all Hungarian
demands which did not directly threaten the unity
of the Monarchy or seriously menace the rights of

the Throne. He was convinced that this Magyar preponderance must be broken in the interests of the Monarchy and the dynasty. As to the way in which this struggle was to be conducted, his opinion varied from time to time. For some time he was wholly in the camp of the Federalists, and directed his efforts to the splitting up of the Monarchy into States possessing equal rights and held together by a strong central government. At another period, especially just before the first Serbian crisis, he inclined to " Trialism " as the best solution. At that period he contemplated the union of the Southern Slavs as an independent State within the Habsburg dominions, but abandoned this scheme when he realized that the union of the Austrian and Hungarian Slavs in a separate national system would merely forward the intentions of the Belgrade Government. Later, strongly influenced by the Hungarian minister Kristoffy, he inclined to the idea of attempting, by a change which would leave the dualism of the Monarchy as such untouched, to strengthen unity by changing the Delegations into a central Parliament and attaching the annexed provinces, Bosnia and Herzegovina, with a State organization of their own, to the Empire.

The opposition which Francis Ferdinand met on all sides from the ruling party in Hungary strengthened his conviction that here lay the essential obstacle to the healthy recovery of the Monarchy. The zeal with which he sought for

the solution of domestic political problems by
strengthening the central power is explained by
his firm conviction that this was the indispensable
condition of the position of the Monarchy as a
Great Power, which he desired to maintain and to
increase.   He was not an unconditional adherent
of the group which thought this aim could only
be attained by force of arms, and he repeatedly
foiled their intentions.   But he was firmly determined to tread this path if it was the only one
by which the goal could be reached.   Personal
inclination and a conviction of the commanding
position of Great Britain made him regard the
establishment of good relations with that Power as
desirable.   Towards the French, and still more
towards the Italians, his attitude was cool and
aloof.   He was convinced that it was impossible
to establish permanently friendly relations with the
Italian nation, and that there must inevitably be
a day of reckoning between the Monarchy and
Italy.   He never adopted an anti-Slav policy.   Not
only did he wish, from the point of view of his
plans for internal reconstruction, to avoid conflicts
with the principal representatives of the Slav
nationalities, but he recognized in the Tsar the
strongest support against revolutionary movements
in monarchical States. Nor is it true that he wanted
to see Serbia struck out of the list of independent
Balkan States ; he merely expressed the decided
opinion that the encroachments of the Greater

Serbia movement on Austro-Hungarian soil should be resisted with all the forces of the Monarchy. He stood faithfully by Germany, with whose ruler his relations became more and more intimate, in spite of the difference between the character of the two men.   Yet no one was less inclined to contemplate the Monarchy falling into a relation of dependence on her powerful ally than Francis Ferdinand, whose whole being was informed with a sense of the majesty of the dynasty.

Francis Ferdinand worked unceasingly for the increase of the defensive power of the Monarchy. He strove to improve the efficiency of the corps of officers, to raise the military spirit among the troops, to increase armaments and to strengthen the fortresses, and he urged that the leading positions of command should be given to energetic men who knew their own minds.   He took a deep interest in the increase of sea power, which ought, in his opinion, to be adapted for operations on a large scale as well as for coast defence, and for this purpose he secured the building of battleships. He was a man of more than average ability.   He had a power of quick comprehension, possessed in a high degree the capacity to recognize the essential point in any business in which he was engaged, and, unlike his uncle, did not allow his general impressions to be clouded by attention to detail. What he lacked was knowledge of men, calmness and constancy in his relations with the men who had been placed in high offices of state by his influence. Beck, Aehrenthal, Conrad, Auffenberg and others lost, not always for any serious reason, the favour of the heir to the Throne as quickly as they had won it. The influence of his wife, ill-natured tittle-tattle to which he listened more and more, and the outbursts of ungovernable rage to which he became increasingly prone with the years, all helped to make intercourse with him more difficult, and prevented a great many persons holding high positions, socially and intellectually, from approaching him. He never enjoyed wide popularity, and, indeed, did not seek it. He asked from the citizens of the Monarchy not affection, but submission to the will of the ruler. For to him the State was identified with the divinely appointed person of the monarch. He understood by *Viribus Unitis* the union of all the forces of the State for the advantage of the Crown, which on its side had to guard the interests of all. This conception accounts for the fact that he took no particular interest in any of the numerous nationalities of the Monarchy. He had undoubtedly German sympathies ; but the German Austrians were to him merely the bulwark of the Throne and of the power of his House. It would never have occurred to him to make dynastic sacrifices for their sake. Even against the Catholic Church, of which he was a convinced adherent, he maintained the rights of the Throne with unbending severity, being in this matter also a true son of the House of Habsburg.

The news of the murder of Francis Ferdinand confirmed the conviction of the necessity for a reckoning with Serbia.   On July 5 the Vienna memorandum was handed to the German Emperor, and on the following day to Bethmann-Hollweg. A Crown Council did not take place ; but authoritative circles in Berlin adopted the views of the Vienna Government and gave it to understand that it might reckon on Germany's assistance even in case international differences were to arise from the Austro-Serbian conflict.

It was in reliance upon these promises, which were repeated by Tschirschky, the German Ambassador at the Court of Vienna, that Berchtold, at the sitting of the Council of Ministers on July 7, 1914, gave utterance to the opinion that they would be forced at last to a military reckoning with Serbia. His point of view met with general agreement. Only Count Tisza, the Hungarian Prime Minister, opposed.   He was without doubt the most eminent politician in the last decades of the old Monarchy— a man of highest power of mind, of irresistible energy, of ardent patriotism, but grievously one-sided and biased ; a man who saw the world only with the eyes of a Magyar noble.   He had already on July 1 expressed his dissent and the reasons for it in a memorandum to the Emperor.   Now in the Council of Ministers he desired not only the

opening of diplomatic negotiations but the formu-
lation of demands possible of fulfilment.   His first
point he carried, but in the second he failed.   The
Council decided to adopt the course of diplomatic
negotiations, but at the same time to lay down
conditions of which the rejection would be inevitable.   In that case the Serbian question would
have to be solved by the power of the sword.
Tisza, ill-content with this conclusion, reiterated
his dissentient views in a second memorandum of
July 8 and counselled moderation, laying stress on
the danger of international complications.   This
view should have been reinforced by the report
drawn up by Friedrich von Wiesner, who had been
sent by the Ballplatz to Sarajevo, on the circumstances in which the attack on the heir to the
Throne had taken place.   This report established
the fact that no direct connection could be proved
between the murderer and the Serbian Government.
But this report failed of its effect.   Authoritative
circles in Vienna remained under the conviction
that the Court and Government of Belgrade had
for a long time past lent their benevolent support
to the Greater Serbia movement, and held to their
determination of putting an end to an unbearable
situation.   The dangers which might arise from
drastic measures were indeed weighed, and even the
possibility of a world war was considered ; but the
opinion prevailed that all must be staked on one card.

It is not at all my purpose to justify the decision

of the Viennese statesmen. They were certainly too hasty. But it must be considered that in all quarters of the realm the opinion prevailed that a Great Power could no longer tolerate the attitude of the Serbian Government. Moreover, twice already a portion of the army had been assembled on the Serbian frontier and had been sent home after standing under arms for several months in the face of the threatening neighbour. Now the military authorities declared that the troops could not be called again to arms without being sure that the differences with Serbia would be settled, if necessary, by the sword. Furthermore, have not nations their sense of honour the same as individuals? Is it therefore so very strange that the Austro-Hungarian statesmen should have thought it impossible to bear any longer the insolence of the Serbs? In this feeling they were actuated by the same sentiments which Lloyd George expressed in the year 1911 in saying that if peace could only be maintained by the dishonour of the British nation, he would not hesitate a moment to take up arms.

"Better a fearful end than endless fears," was the *mot* of a leading Austrian statesman. And these circles were confirmed in their resolve to appeal to arms by the pronouncements of Conrad von Hötzendorf, who in reply to a question announced that the military prospects of the Central Powers in a world war (Great Britain's intervention on the side of the enemy not yet being reckoned with seriously) were no longer so favourable as in previous years, but were certainly more favourable than they would be in the near future.

On July 14 it was decided to send Serbia an ultimatum with a short time-limit. Tisza, after long vacillation, acquiesced, but with the condition that Austria-Hungary was to make a solemn declaration that—with the exception of necessary minor rectifications of the frontier—she sought no territorial gains at the expense of Serbia. By this means he hoped to placate Russia and to deprive the Italians of the pretext for advancing any claim to compensations under Article VII. of the Treaty of the Triple Alliance. This request was indeed taken into account at the conference of ministers of July 19 ; but Berchtold declared that Serbia was to be made smaller and the provinces taken from her were to be divided among some of the other Balkan States. The Note to Serbia, which had only assumed its final form after repeated modification,[1] was read out, and its presentation to the Serbian Government appointed for the afternoon of July 23. Its essential points ran as follows: Since the Great Serbia movement directed against Austria-Hungary has continued in recent years with the ultimate object of separating from the Habsburg Monarchy certain of its parts, and since the

[1] A prominent part in the drafting of the ultimatum was played by Count Forgach and Baron Musulin, who had also, as Berchtold's adviser, a decisive influence on the course of events generally at this time.

Serbian Government, in contradiction to the declaration of March 31, 1909, has not only done nothing towards its suppression but has rather encouraged it, the Austro-Hungarian Government must formulate certain demands in order to put an end to this state of affairs. In these demands are included the condemnation of agitation having as its object the breaking away of portions of the Monarchy and the admonition of the peoples against a continuance of this course: both to be accomplished through an announcement in the official Press organ and through an army order on the part of the King ; the suppression of the Great Serbia agitation on Serbian soil; the dissolution of societies working for this object ; the dismissal of the officials and teachers compromised ; the participation of representatives of the Imperial and Royal Government in the measures which the Serbian Government should be under the obligation to undertake with a view to the suppression of the Great Serbia movement.

The presentation of the Note took place at the appointed time, and on July 24 the world was informed of its contents. Germany alone approved unreservedly. Sazonov broke into a violent outburst, and declared it to be a matter of international concern. Sir Edward Grey described the Note as " the most formidable document " that one State had ever addressed to another. Negotiations began at once between the groups of Powers.

They aimed at the extension of the time-limit of forty-eight hours. England and Russia were especially active in this sense ; but Austria-Hungary refused any prolongation. On July 25, shortly before the expiration of the appointed interval, the Serbs handed in their answer. They declared themselves ready to comply with the majority of the demands, but with regard to certain points—for instance, where it was a question of the participation of the Austro-Hungarian representatives in the judicial inquiry to be held in the territory of the kingdom of Serbia and of the dismissal of the officers and officials who were compromised—certain reservations were made. At the same time they emphasized their willingness to endeavour to reach a friendly solution of the conflict by referring the decision to The Hague Tribunal or to those Great Powers who had collaborated in drafting the Serbian declaration of March 31, 1909. But the Austro-Hungarian Minister, convinced that the Serbs would not keep their promise as they had not kept it before, declared Serbia's answer to be unsatisfactory, and diplomatic relations were broken off.

The Vienna Cabinet's harsh attitude nowhere met with approbation. The German Government itself did not approve it. The Emperor William was of opinion that Austria-Hungary had gained a great moral victory, and that no cause of war remained. But neither his efforts nor those of Sir

Edward Grey, which were directed towards the mediation of the Great Powers not directly involved, met with success. On July 28 Austria-Hungary declared war on Serbia. The Great Powers now strove to localize the conflict, but all their attempts came to nought. Even the English proposal for direct negotiations with a view to an understanding between the Cabinets of Vienna and Petrograd, energetically supported by Germany, led to no result. On the evening of July 29 the order was given for mobilization in the military area on the southwest front of Russia situated on the border of Austria-Hungary. New endeavours of Francis Joseph and William II. to persuade the Tsar to postpone the mobilization of the whole Russian Army failed, owing to the opposition of powerful military and political circles in Petrograd, and likewise the proposal of Sir Edward Grey that the four Great Powers not directly involved should intervene—a suggestion again energetically supported by the German Government. On July 31 the Russian order for a general mobilization was issued, and answered by similar measures on the part of Austria-Hungary and Germany. On August 1, Germany declared war on Russia, and two days after on France ; on August 4, England and Belgium on Germany ; on the 6th, Austria-Hungary on Russia. Other Powers followed suit. The World War, so long dreaded by the Great Powers of Europe, had broken out.

CHAPTER II

THE GREAT WAR
1914-18

THE Central Powers had now to make sure of
the aid of their allies and to win new combatants
to their side. But the efforts which they made
towards this end brought them disappointment
upon disappointment. The conversations which
had taken place with Italy before the outbreak
of the war had made them realize that they could
not reckon on an immediate participation of the
Italian troops. As early as July 25, moreover,
San Giuliano had announced that he would raise
the question of compensation for Italy in case of
an Austro-Serbian war. This announcement he
repeated after the declaration of war, but made it
clear at the same time that Austria-Hungary was
not to expect active support from the Italians,
since she had taken the offensive against Serbia.
Under pressure from the German Government,
which still cherished the hope of inducing Italy,
by far-reaching concessions, to take part in a
world war on the side of the Central Powers,
Berchtold declared himself ready in principle to
recognize the Italian claims to compensation for

every annexation made by Austria-Hungary in the Balkans, but only on the assumption that she would observe a friendly attitude towards the Habsburg Monarchy in an Austro-Serbian war, and in case of a world war fulfil her obligations as a member of the Triple Alliance. But as early as August 1 San Giuliano insisted that the *casus fœderis* had not arisen ; for the time being she would remain neutral, but co-operation with her allies at a later time was referred to as not excluded. It was in the same sense, though in the most cordial terms possible, that Victor Emmanuel answered the telegram in which Francis Joseph expressed his expectation of seeing the Italian troops fighting side by side with those of the Habsburg Monarchy.

Still less gratifying to Vienna were the reports which came in at the same time from Bucharest. The hopes which the Emperor William had built on King Charles's faithfulness to his treaty obligations were not realized. The Rumanian ruler evaded a decisive pronouncement as to his attitude in a world war ; and Bratiano, the Premier, did likewise. Czernin maintained that at first nothing but neutrality could be expected, and insisted that the attitude of the Bulgarians and the Turks, together with the course taken by the events of the war, would be decisive for any further action of the King and Government. It was significant that Bratiano spoke of the necessity of maintaining a balance in the Balkans, and at the same time pointed out the difficulties which would confront the King and the Government in consequence of the hostile attitude of influential Rumanian circles to the Magyars. It was in vain that Francis Joseph and William II. used their personal influence to try and persuade King Charles to take action in the sense they wished. No effect was produced even by the promise made by them to the King on August 2, 1914, that they would help Rumania to obtain possession of Bessarabia after the war had reached a successful conclusion, if she would join in the struggle. The Crown Council held on August 4 decided that Rumania could not admit that the *casus fœderis* had arisen. The assurance given by Charles at the same time, that he would safeguard the Rumanian frontiers and apprise Bulgaria that she would have nothing to fear from Rumania if she ranged herself with the Central Powers, could be of no greater comfort to his disillusioned allies than his solemn declaration that he would never consent to Rumania taking the field against Austria-Hungary.

The Central Powers were rather more fortunate in their quest for new allies than in their attempts to persuade Italy and Rumania to fulfil their engagements. On August 1, 1914, the representatives of Germany and Turkey had signed a treaty by which they bound themselves to remain neutral in the conflict between Austria-Hungary and Serbia ; but the *casus fœderis* would arise at the moment when Russia entered the war. In this event Germany promised Turkey military support, and guaranteed her existing territorial position as against the Russians. By identical notes of August 5, 1914, Austria-Hungary adhered to this treaty, which was to last till the end of 1918. But for the time being the Turks did not actively intervene, for their army was not yet properly equipped and the influence of the friends of the Entente at Constantinople was still too strong. In order to strengthen the Government, which was friendly to the Central Powers, and to make it possible for them shortly to take an active part against the Entente, Germany promised them, as early as the first weeks of August, though only verbally, that in the event of a complete victory of Germany and her allies, their wishes should be furthered both in the matter of the abolition of the Capitulations and of final settlement with Bulgaria ; that all Turkish provinces which might be occupied by the common enemy in the course of the war should be evacuated ; a series of rectifications of the frontier to their advantage would be made and they would receive a proportionate share in the war indemnity which was to be expected. Direct inquiries from the Turks were met by Berchtold with the same promises in the name of Austria-Hungary.

On the other hand, the efforts of the Central Powers to persuade Bulgaria to an alliance broke down. At first, indeed, it looked as if the negotiations which had already been conducted by Austria-Hungary at Sofia for a long time in this sense would speedily lead to a profitable result. Austria-Hungary showed herself inclined, in return for Bulgaria's adhesion to the Triple Alliance, to guarantee her existing territorial possessions, and, in the event of a favourable outcome of the impending conflicts, to gratify Ferdinand's aspirations towards the acquisition of " ethnic-historical boundaries " against States which had not joined the Triple Alliance. By the early days of August, 1914, the negotiations had advanced so far that the signature of the treaties with Germany and Austria-Hungary seemed imminent. Berchtold and Bethmann-Hollweg pressed for a decision, the latter more especially on the ground that he still hoped to win over Rumania definitely to the side of the Central Powers. If this could be achieved, then Bulgaria, assured against attacks from the Rumanian side, might be prompted to draw the sword against Serbia, and the majority of the Austro-Hungarian troops which were marching against Serbia could be diverted against Russia. But Ferdinand of Bulgaria refused to embark on a war against Serbia. He laid stress on the dangers which threatened his kingdom in such a case from Greece, Rumania, and Turkey ;

he also alluded to the large offers which had
been made him by Russia, and held that he
could only come to a decision after his relations
with Rumania and Turkey had been cleared up
and the negotiations for a treaty, which were being
carried on with these Powers, had been concluded. It was clear that Ferdinand of Bulgaria,
too, did not wish to enter the war before the
preponderance of the Central Powers over their
opponents could be assumed with greater confidence. But successes in the field remained to
seek in the Eastern theatre of war. After
promising beginnings, the campaign of the Austro-
Hungarian armies took an unsuccessful turn and
decided Ferdinand to be prudent. He declared
that he would remain neutral, but for the present
he could do no more.

The ill success of the Austro-Hungarian armies
did not produce an effect on the Bulgarian Government alone. With the advance of the Russians
and their approach to the Rumanian frontiers,
the influence of the friends of the Entente at
Bucharest increased. The news arriving at
Berlin and Vienna at this time caused the worst
to be feared. It was believed that an overthrow
of the dynasty was imminent, together with an
immediate alliance of Rumania with the enemy
and an advance of Rumanian troops into Transylvania. The most pressing advice reached Vienna
from Berlin in favour of far-reaching concessions,

even of a territorial nature. But, strongly influenced by Tisza, Berchtold refused any concessions in this direction. Under the advice of King Charles, who was already seriously ill and was torn by a terrible conflict between personal honour and the wishes of his people, the Central Powers sought to work upon public opinion in Bucharest by a declaration that the defection of Rumania would be met by an immediate advance of troops into the country. But their threats remained ineffectual, for it was known in Bucharest that the troops necessary for such an enterprise were not forthcoming. In reality, Germany was counselling Vienna not to oppose the march of Rumanian troops into Transylvania by force of arms, since for the moment a defence of the frontiers was impossible, but rather to tolerate the advance, and to announce that it had taken place in order to defend the territory from occupation by Russian troops. Berchtold refused, and Tisza, whose acrimony over the German proposal knew no bounds, declared that he would rather see the Russians than the Rumanians in Transylvania. Meanwhile the tide of warlike enthusiasm at Bucharest mounted higher and higher. The Government entered on September 23 into a written agreement with Italy providing for common action. A Crown Council was summoned for the early days of October, which was to come to a decision against the Central Powers. Only at the last moment was it possible to avert the danger. The Council was cancelled, and Rumania for the time being remained neutral. A few days later, on October 10, King Charles died. He had not fulfilled the engagements into which he had entered, but he had at least prevented his troops from fighting against the Central Powers.

One of the chief reasons which had delayed Rumania in going over to the camp of the Entente was the fear that so soon as her troops had crossed the Hungarian frontier Bulgaria and Turkey would attack her. The negotiations carried on through the intermediary of Austria-Hungary between Sofia and Bucharest had, it is true, been proceeded with, but had broken down again, this time owing to the distrust and the irreconcilable interests of the two Powers. At the same time it had become known in Bucharest how closely the Turks had attached themselves to the Central Powers, and that they were holding themselves in readiness to enter the war on their side. Rumania consequently declared that she could no longer leave Bulgaria a free hand against Serbia. Thus under the new King of Rumania, Ferdinand, who was not bound by ties of personal friendship with the sovereigns of Austria-Hungary and Germany, the party hostile to the Central Powers gained in influence. Ferdinand did indeed stand firm in his neutrality, and he rejected Russia's summons to hasten to the aid of the

Serbians, who had been attacked by Austria-Hungary. But Czernin could not succeed in obtaining from him a binding declaration that he would not let his troops enter the field against the Central Powers.

At this time Germany and Austria-Hungary were equally powerless to decide the King of Bulgaria to take part in the Serbian war. Even the increased inducements held out to him in this event by the Vienna Government did not move him from this attitude of reserve. This was due not only to his distrust of Rumania, Greece and Turkey and his fear of Russia, but also to his doubt as to whether by joining the Central Powers he would really be placing himself on the winning side. Accordingly, he was forever changing his attitude according to the vicissitudes of the war. If the armies of the Central Powers met with success, they all showed a growing inclination to bring the treaty negotiations, which had never been allowed to drop, to a conclusion. But if, as in December, 1914, unfavourable news reached Sofia as to the military situation of the Central Powers, the old reasons for dragging on the negotiations were raked up again. The fact that the Entente Powers kept going further and further in their offers to Bulgaria, should she enter the war on their side or even should she remain neutral, contributed towards strengthening the resolve of the Bulgarian Government to put the

screw on the Central Powers. Thus at the end
of 1914 they demanded far-reaching concessions
in the matter of their territorial claims, and that
under a written promise. Austria-Hungary was
refractory for a time, but at the beginning of
1915 declared herself prepared even for these
concessions, demanding, however, with the backing
of the German Government, the armed intervention of Bulgaria on the side of the Central
Powers. But neither King Ferdinand of Bulgaria
nor Radoslavov, the Bulgarian Premier, was
willing to concede this, for the military situation
of the Central Powers was for the moment unfavourable, and they declared their wish to remain neutral.

The negotiations with Rumania and Bulgaria
revealed the fact that both Powers, different
though their interests might be, followed a
similar policy. They wished to delay their decision
as long as possible ; they wished at the right
moment to join the side of the winning party,
so as to carry off the greatest possible advantage
at the price of the least possible sacrifices. In
these circumstances, the importance to the outcome of the war of Italy's decision increased
every month. For a long time, until far on in
the winter of 1914, the policy of leading Italian
statesmen was dictated by the wish to preserve
their neutrality while continuing their preparations. They accounted for their attitude by

referring to the letter and the spirit of the Triple
Alliance ; they gave their former allies friendly
words, but maintained a cordial attitude towards
the Entente Powers.   At the same time they
urged at Vienna their demands for compensations by interpreting Article VII. of the Triple
Alliance Treaty in their own favour.   It was not
at first clear what they meant by it.   During
the official negotiations which took place between
the Cabinets of Vienna and Rome, no word was
spoken on the Italian side of old Austrian
territories.   But it was learned at the Ballplatz,
by way of Berlin, that Italy was thinking of the
Trentino.   Berchtold absolutely refused to listen
to any such demands.   He would not hear of a
territorial indemnification, and was warmly supported by Tisza, while Conrad even at that time,
or at any rate in times of military misfortune,
considered that even Italian neutrality would not
be too dearly bought at the price of great
sacrifices.   But neither the prayers of the leading
military commander nor the unceasing efforts of
leading German political and military circles were
able to change Berchtold's mind.   He continued
the negotiations, but spun them out without binding
himself to anything.

When San Giuliano died on October 16, 1914,
nothing decisive had yet happened.   Even during
the few weeks for which Salandra, the then
Italian Premier, directed Italy's foreign policy,

no energetic steps were taken. Salandra followed the feeling of the country, which changed according to the success of either party in the war. It was not until Sonnino had taken control of foreign affairs that a further advance was ventured on, in view of the unfavourable military position of the Central Powers, and under the influence of the section of the Italian Press which was active in the interest of the Entente. It was once more reported in Vienna that Sonnino had spoken in Berlin of the cession of the Trentino, and that the German Government was now advocating this sacrifice. But even now Berchtold refused to entertain the question. Francis Joseph, so it was said, would never give his consent to a diminution of his Empire. But Sonnino kept on his way unperturbed. At the beginning of December, 1914—when Austria-Hungary was advancing upon Serbia—he made a declaration at Vienna to the effect that the excited state of opinion in Italy compelled him to press for the adjustment of the question of compensations. Salandra supported him by speaking in Parliament of Italy's *sacro egoismo*, her just aspirations and legitimate interests, and while giving expression to the pacific character of the Italian Government, he stated emphatically that neutrality alone was not sufficient to assure Italy's interests in all circumstances until the end of the war.

In the middle of December the negotiations

between Vienna and Rome began afresh, but at
once came to a deadlock. The German Government, which attached extraordinary importance to
winning over Italy, now tried to persuade the
Ballplatz to make concessions. At the same time
it sent to Rome Prince Bülow, who worked in
the same sense, and represented concessions on
the part of Austria-Hungary as a sacrifice, heavy
indeed, but necessary to assure Italy's neutrality.
But Berchtold was still resolutely opposed to such
a demand, and expressed this view also in his
direct negotiations with the Italian Ambassador
in Vienna, the Duke of Avarna.

On January 13, 1915, Berchtold was removed
and Baron Burian succeeded him as Austro-
Hungarian Foreign Minister. Burian was, by
universal consent, a man of high culture and great
knowledge ; he was extremely well informed in
the countries and the life of the Near East. But
there was something of the professor and the
doctrinaire in his character. He studied very
thoroughly every question which he had to decide,
and took all the circumstances into consideration
before forming an opinion. But nothing, not even
the most convincing arguments, would turn him
from an opinion once formed ; indeed, according
to the testimony of those who worked with him,
he regarded even the most reasonable opposition
as a personal affront. Burian continued negotiations with Italy, but they led at first to no

rapprochement between the two opposing points of view.   It was not till March 9, 1915, that he expressed his willingness to discuss with Italy, in principle, the cession of Austrian territory.   He did so under the impression of the unfavourable military position of the Triple Alliance Powers— the Russians were fighting in the Carpathians, and Przemysl was about to fall—and with the knowledge of the renewal in February of the agreement between Italy and Rumania, which suggested that a declaration of war by Italy would be followed by that of Rumania ; under increasingly heavy pressure, moreover, from the German Government, which, in the event of a favourable outcome of the war, held before the eyes of the Vienna Government, as compensations for the losses of the Monarchy in Tyrol, not only a loan in cash, but also the rich coal mines of Sosnovica.

The opening of negotiations at once showed how far the Italian demands exceeded what Austria-Hungary was prepared to concede.   Sonnino asked for wide territories and their immediate transfer to the Italians.   Burian firmly refused the latter proposal, and only offered the greater part of Italian Southern Tyrol, and even this on condition that Italy should preserve a benevolent neutrality towards the Central Powers until the end of the war and leave Austria-Hungary a free hand in the Balkans.   Sonnino rejected the offer as in-

6

sufficient, and during the next few weeks increased his demands.   On April 10, on Sonnino's instructions, a memorandum containing Italy's new conditions was handed in at Vienna.   They made it clear that Italy was no longer striving to complete her national growth while preserving her former relations with the Habsburg Monarchy, but was aiming at the realization of her national unity and at the achievement of complete supremacy in the Adriatic.   She demanded, among other things, the whole of South Tyrol, with the boundaries of the Italian Kingdom of 1811, Gorizia and Gradiska, and the conversion of Trieste with its surrounding territory into a community independent of Austria-Hungary ; the cession of a number of the most important islands in the Adriatic ; the immediate occupation of these lands by the Italians ; the recognition of the full sovereignty over Valona and its territory ;. and a declaration of Austria-Hungary's *désinteressement* as regards Albania.   In return, Italy was prepared to promise neutrality for the duration of the war, and to renounce, but only for this period, the construction in her own favour of the provisions of the Triple Alliance Treaty.

In spite of the enormity of these demands, they were not flatly refused by Burian, since the military situation compelled him to continue negotiations, and German statesmen and Generals pointed out to him the disastrous consequences which would follow if Italy went over into the enemy camp. The fall of Constantinople was threatening, the Russians were pressing relentlessly forward, Hungary seemed at their mercy, and it might happen that a declaration of war by Italy would be followed by Rumania, and even by Bulgaria. Then the hemming in of the Central Powers would be complete and the seal would be placed upon their ruin. Burian could not cast doubt upon these arguments ; it was not without influence upon him that Conrad now advocated every concession to Italy. Burian therefore increased his concessions, but did not yield all that Italy demanded. He retreated, rather, step by step, always led by the hope that a new turn would be given to events in the theatre of war, and sought to hold the Italians without rebuffing them. But since the latter did not count upon securing their demands from Vienna, and were convinced that the Habsburg Monarchy would recover what had been squeezed from it in the hour of need, should the military situation take a more favourable turn, they determined to bring to a conclusion the negotiations which they had long carried on with the Entente Powers. On April 26, 1915, the Treaty of London was signed, which pledged Italy to enter the war by the side of her new allies at the end of a month, and contained the assurance of an extension of territory going far beyond

that which she had demanded from Austria-
Hungary at the price of maintaining neutrality.

Having come to terms with the Entente Powers,
Italy resumed negotiations with Vienna, not with
the intention of pursuing them to any profitable
end, but rather in order to find in the refusal
of her demands grounds for going over to the
enemy camp and time to complete her warlike
preparations. It was, therefore, in vain that
Burian, under pressure of the Austro-Hungarian
and German Army Commands and of the German
Government, went further and further in concessions. On April 21 Sonnino declared that the
points of view were too wide apart, and on
April 25 the Duke of Avarna, the Italian Ambassador, who had up till then worked untiringly
for a friendly understanding, expressed his opinion
that a breach was inevitable. Even Prince Bülow,
who continued the negotiations at Rome up to
the last moment, let it be understood that he
no longer believed the Italians to be in earnest
in seeking a compromise. On May 3, in fact,
Italy resolved to denounce the alliance with
Austria and to claim full freedom of action. In
vain the Vienna Cabinet made yet further concessions, which now included almost everything
that the Italians had demanded. Sonnino continued indeed to negotiate, but he was always
finding fresh reasons for postponing a decision.
On May 20 the Italian Government received from

the Chambers the extraordinary powers necessitated by the approaching conflict, and on the 23rd war was declared on Austria-Hungary.

One of the chief reasons which had decided Burian to offer such far-reaching concessions to Italy in April and May was the pressure from the military Higher Command, and especially from Conrad, who never ceased to insist in his memoranda that Italy's entry into the war would be followed by that of Rumania, and on this account adjured Burian to make every sacrifice in order to avert the otherwise unavoidable catastrophe by winning over Italy. Czernin, too, expressed himself in a like sense, since King Ferdinand had at the beginning of March admitted to him that in the event of Italy taking sides against Austria-Hungary, he would be bound to follow her example. That his fears were well grounded was the less doubtful, since it was already known in Vienna that on February 6 the agreement concluded in September, 1914, between Italy and Rumania had been renewed for four months, and had received an extension to the effect that the two Governments bound themselves to render each other aid in the event of an unprovoked attack on the part of Austria-Hungary. The negotiations as to the cession of Austrian territory, which had been begun with Italy under the impression of this news, had now as their result that Rumania too raised the price of her continued neutrality.

It was no longer only the Bukovina that was mentioned, but also Transylvania. But Tisza declared that he would not sacrifice a square yard of Hungarian soil, and the Vienna Cabinet agreed with him. The result was an increase of the influence of the Triple Entente in Rumania, which was further heightened by Russia's victories in the Carpathians and the breakdown of the negotiations between Burian and Sonnino. The climax of hostility to the Central Powers in Bucharest was reached on April 27, when the Italian Minister announced a declaration of war on the Habsburg Monarchy to be unavoidable. Czernin expressed his conviction that Rumania would declare war forty-eight hours after Italy. Only one thing could restrain Rumania—a great victory of the Central Powers over the Russians. And this now happened in the break through at Gorlice on May 2. Its effect was felt at once. Bratiano now declared that the position was indeed very critical, but that he hoped to maintain neutrality ; and further news of the successes of the German and Austro-Hungarian troops in Galicia and Poland contributed towards strengthening the Rumanian Government in their resolve not to give up their neutrality for the present. In these circumstances even the Italian declaration of war did not alter the Rumanian position ; but the altered conditions of the war certainly influenced the attitude of the Vienna Government. Its interest in Rumania now sensibly declined, since her neutrality seemed assured by the military situation.

The desire of the Central Powers to arrive at a decision in their negotiations with Bulgaria became all the more urgent. Since January the Turks had been successfully defending the Dardanelles against the attacks of the allied Western Powers ; but their position was menaced by the fact that they lacked arms and munitions, which Germany had bound herself to provide by the terms of a treaty concluded on January 11, with which Austria-Hungary associated herself on March 21. It was therefore necessary to establish secure communications with the Turks ; and, since all the efforts of the Central Powers to obtain the transport of arms and munitions through Rumania remained fruitless, it was necessary to try and make sure of a way through Bulgaria into Turkish territory. The adherence of Bulgaria would also produce a further advantage. With Bulgaria in alliance with the Central Powers, Rumania would be less inclined to risk joining their enemies, since in that case she would have to reckon with Bulgaria, who had not forgiven the wounds inflicted by the Treaty of Bucharest in 1913.

It was not an easy matter for the Cabinets of Vienna and Berlin to win over the Bulgarians. Both the King and Radoslavov distrusted the Rumanians and Turks and feared the Greeks and

Russians.   Moreover, the far-reaching offers of
the Entente Powers were not without influence
upon them.   Their attitude in their dealings with
the representatives of the Central Powers was
guarded, and they kept increasing their demands.
As early as the end of 1914 the Vienna Government, in view of the unfavourable military position
in Serbia and Galicia, and in consequence of the
pressure exerted upon it not only by the German
politicians and military commanders but also by
Conrad, had declared its readiness to concede to
the Bulgarians, in the event of their entry into
the war on the side of the Central Powers, the
possession of those Serbian territories to which
they advanced historical and ethnographical claims
—only, however, so far as they should occupy them
with their own troops during the course of the war.
The negotiations started at the beginning of 1915
on this basis were protracted by the Bulgarians ;
for, in view of the unfavourable military situation
of the Central Powers at the time, King Ferdinand
and Radoslavov did not think it expedient to enter
into permanent engagements.   They therefore declared that they could only promise to remain
neutral, but demanded in return considerable
extensions of territory in Macedonia, increasing
their claims in March and April under the impression of the Russian victories in the Carpathians and the danger threatening Turkey from
the Western Powers.

Burian, however, held firmly to the position
that he could only make territorial concessions
in return for active participation on Bulgaria's
part. The break through at Gorlice and the subsequent victorious advance of the German and
Austro-Hungarian troops also produced their effect
in Sofia. The negotiations with the Central
Powers were carried on with more zeal ; but they
failed to reach a settlement, since the demands
of the Bulgarians continued to be out of all proportion to any services which they seemed disposed
to offer in return. They declined to attack Serbia,
refused a military convention proposed to them
by the Central Powers, but at the same time increased the price of their continued neutrality.
The entry of Italy into the war, and the increasingly
extensive offers on the part of the Entente, added
to the difficulty of the negotiations between Vienna
and Sofia. But gradually the conviction gained
ground in Sofia that adherence to the Central
Powers would serve the interests of Bulgaria
better than an alliance with the Entente. For
it would be easy for the former to concede the
extensions of territory desired by Bulgaria in
Macedonia at Serbia's expense, whereas the Entente
Powers were bound to fear that similar concessions on their part would give offence to their
faithful ally. The Triple Entente failed in their
efforts to persuade the Serbs to consent to this
sacrifice by promising them, in the event of

ultimate victory, the possession of Bosnia, Herzegovina and Dalmatia ; for Bulgaria demanded immediate possession of the Macedonian territories promised her, while Serbia wanted the transfer of these territories to be postponed until she herself should have secured the extension of territory promised to her by way of compensation.

It was only when the continued advances of the Germans and Austro-Hungarians in Poland made the prospects of the ultimate victory of the Central Powers seem very favourable that the advantage to be gained by joining them was definitely recognized at Sofia. From July onwards negotiations were energetically carried on. The Central Powers insisted on the signature of a military convention in addition to the treaty of alliance, and that Bulgaria should at the same time conclude a treaty with the Turks. After innumerable difficulties had been surmounted, the treaties between Austria-Hungary and Bulgaria were signed on September 6. The most important article contained a guarantee by Austria-Hungary of the independence and integrity of Bulgaria against any attack not provoked by Bulgaria herself, this guarantee to be valid for the duration of the alliance, i.e. till December 31, 1920, and after that for a year, and so on until the treaty should be denounced in proper form. Bulgaria, for her part, undertook to give Austria-Hungary proportionate armed assistance in the event of the

Monarchy being attacked by a State bordering on Bulgaria and demanding her aid. The second agreement, signed on the same day, contained a pledge from Bulgaria that she would take the offensive against Serbia, in return for which, what is now Serbian Macedonia, the so-called " disputed " and " non-disputed " zones, as established by the Serbo-Bulgarian Treaty of March 13, 1912—was promised to her. In the meantime it was agreed that, in the event of an attack by Rumania on Bulgaria or her allies—including the Turks—which should not have been provoked by Bulgaria, Austria-Hungary would consent to the recovery by Bulgaria of the territory ceded by her to Rumania by the Peace of Bucharest, and a rectification of the Rumano-Bulgarian frontier as defined by the Treaty of Berlin. A similar promise was made to Bulgaria, under the same conditions, with regard to the territory ceded by her to Greece by the Peace of Bucharest. The military convention signed on the same day settled the provisions for the carrying out of the impending joint offensive against Serbia. The negotiations between the Turks and Bulgarians, which had been going on for a year, were also brought to a conclusion on September 6, thanks to persistent pressure from the Central Powers. Turkey yielded on the essential point by agreeing to a rectification of the frontier in favour of Bulgaria on both banks of the Maritza.

The significance of the adhesion of Bulgaria to the Central Powers lay in the fact that it secured their communications with Turkey, which was of extreme importance, and also the possibility of a victorious campaign against Serbia. The campaign now began and proceeded according to programme. Though valiantly defended by the Serbs against overwhelming numbers, their country fell, towards the end of 1915, into the hands of the Central Powers and Bulgaria. Shortly afterwards Montenegro shared the same fate.

The year 1915 also brought " Congress Poland " into the power of the Central Powers. After the fall of Warsaw on August 5, 1915, governments were set up on behalf of Germany at Warsaw and on behalf of Austria-Hungary at Lublin, to which all powers were handed over. At first the Central Powers had not contemplated the permanent acquisition of " Congress Poland." It was merely considered as a pawn and an item for compensation at the end of the war. But after the fall of Warsaw the Cabinets of Vienna and Berlin tried to arrive at an agreement as to the future destiny of Poland. The most various solutions were discussed, but no definite agreement was reached. The idea of handing Poland back to Russia was indeed repeatedly advanced by Germany—both in the year 1915 and again very actively after July, 1916—when Stürmer directed foreign affairs in the empire of the Tsar. But since the condition of such a solution—namely, a total separation of Russia from the Entente—could not be brought about, it was allowed to drop. The plan of dividing the whole of the conquered territory of Poland between Austria-Hungary and Germany was also considered. But insuperable difficulties arose in the course of the negotiations, particularly with regard to the frontiers of the respective territories. It was also foreseen that the Poles would not voluntarily submit to a new partition of their country and that they would struggle for its reunion. It was feared, moreover, that far-reaching differences between the allies would be revealed the moment economic and military questions should come under discussion. The idea of annexing "Congress Poland" to Germany, first ventilated by a section of public opinion and in military circles in Germany, was rejected not only by the Vienna Cabinet but also by the German Chancellor, since he feared the increase of Polish influence in Germany. The plan advocated for a time by Bethmann-Hollweg of founding an independent Polish buffer State, which should be in economic, political and military alliance with the Central Powers, also split upon the opposition of the Vienna Government.

Thus the union of "Congress Poland" with the Habsburg Monarchy, which Burian had proposed in August, 1915, and which had been advocated by the writings of Count Andrassy among others, stood out more clearly as the only possible solution of the Polish question. But this too presented great difficulties on closer examination. There were adherents of the idea of a personal union, and on the other hand of an actual union ; among the latter were those who were in favour of a trialistic form for the new greater Austria-Hungary, and those who advocated the incorporation of Poland in the Austrian State. Under the influence of the Hungarian Government, whose spokesman, Count Tisza, protested in the strongest terms against the organization of the Monarchy on a trialistic basis, the idea now prevailed of annexing Poland to Austria-Hungary and granting to the united territory of Poland, with the addition of Galicia, a far-reaching autonomy. This had the further object of diminishing the damage to the interests of the German Austrians which was feared by wide circles in Austria and Germany. Since the autumn of 1915 negotiations were carried on between leading statesmen of Germany and Austria-Hungary on this basis. But the more deeply the question was considered, the greater were the difficulties which presented themselves. Bethmann-Hollweg declared that the German people could only agree to such a strengthening of Austria-Hungary in the event of the German Empire coming out of the war with an equally large increase of territory. Economic and military objections were also advanced on the German side, and as a solution it was proposed to incorporate a small portion of " Congress Poland " with Austrian Galicia, and out of the greater part of the rest to create a Polish State independent in form, but in reality under the protectorate of Germany. But this proposal was firmly rejected by the Vienna Government, which advanced the idea of a genuinely autonomous State comprising the whole of Polish territory, which should be allied by a long-term economic and military agreement with both the Central Powers equally. But it was impossible to win the consent of the Berlin Government to this plan.

Such was the position when the Austro-Hungarian troops were defeated at Lutsk. The result of this was that in August, 1916, the Germans carried the day with their proposal to found an independent State, practically comprising the former " Congress Poland," under a hereditary constitutional monarchy, but subject to far-reaching restrictions in military and economic matters. On the Austro-Hungarian side the bestowal of the crown of Poland on a member of the family of Habsburg-Lorraine was waived. A more exact definition of the sphere of influence of the Central Powers was reserved for further discussion. But their subsequent course showed that the opposition of interests was too deep-seated for it to be possible to settle matters in a hurry. In October,

1916, therefore, they came to a settlement for the present to shelve the question of an independent Polish State. But in order to calm the Poles, who were anxious about their fate, and to secure the assistance of their armed forces for the Central Powers, a proclamation was issued on November 5, 1916, in which a prospect was held out of the restoration of an independent Poland as a hereditary constitutional monarchy closely attached to the Central Powers. But the two military governments at Warsaw and Lublin continued to administer the country.

Even before this agreement had been arrived at, Rumania had gone over to the Entente camp. The Central Powers had indeed not been wanting in offers to the Rumanian Government between Italy's entry into the war and the conclusion of the treaties with Bulgaria ; but they had made their concessions conditional on the active intervention of Rumania on their side. The leading statesmen of Bucharest would not agree to this ; for, in spite of the great military success of the Central Powers, their final victory seemed doubtful. They accordingly continued to insist on important cessions of territory in the Bukovina and Transylvania by Austria-Hungary in return for a continuance of their neutrality. To this, however, Burian, strongly influenced by Tisza, refused to agree, although not only the German Government but also Conrad von

Hötzendorf actively supported Rumania's demands. Thus the negotiations, which had been reluctantly continued by Burian, remained without results. Even Bulgaria's adhesion to the Central Powers, and the successful campaign against Serbia, did not produce any change in the attitude of the two Governments. The majority of Rumanian politicians counted on a rapid change in the military situation, and the Entente diplomatists made every effort to confirm them in this belief. But the Rumanian Government maintained its conviction that it must for the present preserve its neutrality. It was the Russian victories at Lutsk and Okna which first led to a change in their views. At the end of June, 1916, the Vienna Cabinet was aware, from its Ambassador, Count Czernin, that preparations for war were being completed in Bucharest, that negotiations were being carried on with the Entente Powers as to the conditions of going over to them, and that the probability was that Rumania would draw the sword after the harvest.

In spite of this, and though the news during the next few weeks was more and more unfavourable, Burian firmly refused the demands made by Rumania for the maintenance of neutrality, and was not to be moved from his resolve even by the German Government and Conrad von Hötzendorf. And so towards the end of August the union of Rumania with the Entente Powers was accomplished, in return for far-reaching territorial concessions granted by them to their new ally at the expense of the Austro-Hungarian Monarchy. On August 27—on the day of Italy's formal rupture with Germany—followed Rumania's declaration of war on Austria-Hungary, and hostilities began without delay. But the hope of the Entente that Rumania's entry on their side would quickly decide the war in their favour was not fulfilled. After preliminary Rumanian successes against the weak troops of the Habsburg Monarchy, the armies of the Quadruple Alliance, fighting under German leadership, achieved a decisive victory. On December 6, 1916, Bucharest was taken, and at the beginning of January, 1917, two-thirds of Rumania was occupied.

Turkey's danger had grown through the entry of Rumania into the war, and she now addressed herself to the Central Powers with fresh demands. On September 28 Germany assured the Porte that, in accordance with her treaty engagements, she would not conclude a separate peace, would allow Turkey a share, proportionate to her military efforts, in any territorial conquests, and would not agree to any peace so long as Turkish territory was occupied by the enemy. Soon afterwards, on January 11, 1917, a further agreement was arrived at, in which the abolition of the Capitulations, which Turkey found oppressive, was contemplated. The provisions of these two treaties were expanded in a manner favourable to Turkey on November 27, 1917. The Austro-Hungarian Government, after long hesitation, associated itself on March 22, 1917, with the German agreements, but her ratification was withheld. A treaty was signed between Austria-Hungary and Turkey on May 30, 1918, relating to the Capitulations, which corresponded to the Turko-German treaty of November 27, 1917, and by which Austria-Hungary pledged herself not to sign any peace which should re-establish the Capitulations.

The success of the Central Powers in Rumania was a ray of light in the last days of the Emperor Francis Joseph, who had entered the war with a heavy heart and remained full of anxiety as to the fate of his Empire. At the outbreak of the war he expressed his opinion that he would be very happy if Austria-Hungary got off with a black eye and no bones broken. His armies and those of his allies had achieved decisive victories in several theatres of war in the course of the year 1916 ; they had occupied new territories, and in other quarters had successfully repelled the increasingly formidable offensive of their enemies. The battles on the Isonzo had thrown the heroism of the Austro-Hungarian troops into particularly clear relief. But the number and military efficiency of their enemies increased, and since Great Britain commanded the sea and the United States supported them more and more

lavishly, the Entente armies had at their disposition vast masses of arms and munitions of every
kind, and also immense supplies of food-stuffs. The
Central Powers, thrown back upon their own
industrial resources and hampered in the import
of food-stuffs and the production of weapons by
the British blockade, could not keep pace.

For this reason the desire to put an end to
the internecine struggle of the nations grew from
month to month, especially in Austria-Hungary,
where from the beginning of the war a great part
of the population had only fought unwillingly for
interests which were not regarded as their own.
In the course of the year 1914 Francis Joseph
had not refused to listen to suggestions for a peace
which should take into account the most important
interests of his Empire, and he had approved
the numerous proposals for peace which in the
years 1915–16 had come from more or less
authoritative quarters ; but he had always insisted
most strongly that these negotiations must be conducted in full agreement with his allies, and
especially with Germany.   But all these peace
proposals had proved abortive, since neither
Germany nor Austria-Hungary saw the possibility
of ending the war on any terms commensurate with
the military situation and their desires.   But in
October, 1916, in order to prove to the public
opinion of the world that it was not the insatiability
of the Central Powers which stood in the way of

peace, Burian proposed to the German Imperial Chancellor, at the general headquarters at Pless, that the Quadruple Alliance should inform their enemies, through neutral channels, of their conditions of peace, and also publish them, in order to enlighten their own peoples as to their war aims and win over the neutral Powers to an active intervention with the enemy Governments. Bethmann-Hollweg and the other German statesmen agreed in principle, but they declined to communicate their peace conditions, since they felt themselves bound, especially in the Belgian question, to advance demands which their enemies, and especially Great Britain, could not possibly accept.

On this point excited debates and serious conflicts took place between the Vienna and Berlin Cabinets, in the course of which the Austrians demanded the recall of Tschirschky, the German Ambassador at the Court of Vienna, who represented the German point of view with uncompromising harshness. Even the sovereigns of Austria-Hungary and Germany took part in this conflict. The Emperor William sought insistently to convince his ally that Germany could not fall in with Burian's plan. It was one of Francis Joseph's last acts to invoke every means in order to accomplish a settlement of the outstanding difficulties. It was only after long negotiations—Francis Joseph having in the meantime died on

November 21—that it was possible to reach a compromise. It was agreed to submit the proposal of the Quadruple Alliance to their enemies through the neutral Powers, and immediately to enter upon deliberations as to a peace, in the course of which their peace conditions should be exactly defined.

The death of Francis Joseph and the accession of the Emperor Charles to the throne of Austria-Hungary notably reinforced the peace party at Vienna. Seldom has a ruler on ascending the throne been faced with a more difficult situation. The struggle between the nations had been going on for more than two years. For more than two years the troops of the Monarchy had been fighting heroically against the superior forces of their enemies. The military and economic resources of the Monarchy were beginning to fail. Behind the front, especially in the towns of Austria, there was lack of the necessaries of life, and already it was clear that anti-dynastic feeling was spreading, especially in the non-German and non-Magyar territories. His programme was to combat this feeling, to renew the splendour of the dynasty, to give to the peoples under his rule the longed-for peace, and to bring about a settlement between the different nations composing the Habsburg Monarchy. But he had not the energy and strength of character necessary to carry out his views. Even his adherents, while praising his powerful memory, his gift of rapid comprehension, his marked sense of the greatness of his House, his devotion to duty and his personal charm, admit that he lacked the stronger qualities which would have been necessary to find the right path.

In his first declarations Charles emphasized his firm intention of doing everything in his power to put an end to the terrible conflict. In this attitude he was strongly confirmed by his wife Zita, by her mother, the influential Maria Antonia of Parma, and by his brothers-in-law, Sixtus and Xavier, who, as early as November, 1916, tried to get in touch with the Entente Powers. On December 12 the peace offer of the Quadruple Alliance was made public. It contained a promise to submit to a conference of the Powers proposals which should aim at assuring to their peoples existence, honour and freedom of development, and at laying foundations calculated to estab- lish a lasting peace. In conversations with Germany, Austria-Hungary defined her stand- point. She claimed the integrity of her territory, trifling frontier rectifications as against Russia, a more favourable strategic frontier against Rumania, the cession to Austria-Hungary of a small portion of the territory of the Serbian monarchy and of larger portions to Bulgaria and Albania, and a more favourable strategic frontier against Italy ; in addition to this the economic union of Serbia with the Habsburg Monarchy, and Albanian autonomy under an Austro-Hungarian

Protectorate. Independently of the peace activity of the Quadruple Alliance, Woodrow Wilson, on December 18, invited the belligerent Powers to communicate their peace terms. Both proposals, however, were declined by the Entente Powers. On December 30, Briand, on the part of France, declared the peace offer of the Quadruple Alliance to be a war manœuvre, and that all negotiations were useless, so long as no security was given for the restoration of violated rights and liberties and the recognition of the right of peoples to self-determination. In the Note drawn up in concert by the Entente Powers on January 12, 1917, in answer to President Wilson's communication, all the blame for the outbreak of war was imputed to the Central Powers, and the demand was formulated, among other things, for compensation for all war damages, the restoration of Alsace-Lorraine to France, and from Austria-Hungary proportionate cessions of territory to Italy as well. The German Government, which had by now fallen into more and more obvious dependence on the Higher Army Command, thereupon resolved to carry on the war by the employment of the most extreme measures, the most important and most promising of which was indicated in authoritative quarters to be unlimited submarine warfare.

Baron Burian, meanwhile, had ceased to be Austro-Hungarian Foreign Minister on December

22, 1916, and was succeeded by Count Ottokar Czernin, the former Ambassador at Bucharest. Estimates of Czernin differ. That he possesses ability far above the average is recognized. He is an accomplished speaker and a clever writer, who is able to arrest the attention of his hearers and his readers. A thoroughly modern man who understood that times change and was willing to change with them, he showed greater inclination than most of his class to meet the wishes of the aspiring democracy. His enemies reproach him with untrustworthiness, dilettantism and pride ; friend and foe alike lay stress on the irritability of his nervous system as accounting for the " jumpiness " of his disposition. Austro-Hungarian statesmen generally did not share the exaggerated expectations of German military circles as to the effects of the submarine campaign. Czernin, in particular, gave open expression to his doubts about the subjugation of England within a few months, which the German authorities seemed to regard as certain ; and he drew attention to the danger of an active intervention of the United States. The Emperor shared his Minister's views. But the continual pressure of German statesmen and the German Higher Command, powerfully supported by the Emperor William, at last succeeded in obtaining the consent of the Austro-Hungarian Government to unlimited submarine warfare. The war was resumed by Germany and her allies by land, by sea and in the air, but the hope of forcing their enemies to their knees by decisive successes was not realized. During the year 1917 there were, indeed, moments in which it looked as if the final decision would be in their favour. But their enemies, in spite of all the successes of the Central Powers and their allies, held firmly to their belief that time would work in their favour, and even in moments of greatest danger rejected all thoughts of a peace unsatisfactory to them. What confirmed them chiefly in this attitude was the hope of military assistance from the United States.

The opening of unlimited submarine warfare was followed immediately by the rupture of diplomatic relations between the Cabinets of Berlin and Washington, and on April 5 by the declaration of war on Germany by the United States. It was not until December 7, 1917, that the United States declared war on Austria-Hungary. Meanwhile, since the successes of the submarine warfare, though in themselves considerable, did not produce the result foretold by Germany, the Emperor Charles's inclination towards peace grew from month to month. Under the influence of his entourage he determined, by secret negotiations with the enemy, to work for a peace which should include a guarantee of the integrity of the Habsburg Monarchy by the Entente Powers. His brother-in-law, Prince Sixtus of Bourbon

Parma, undertook the rôle of mediator, and on March 24 Charles empowered him, by letter, to declare to M. Poincaré that in order to obtain peace he would exert every effort in his power to support the just claims of France to Alsace-Lorraine. In other questions, too, notably in that of Belgium, the Emperor showed a wish to further the desires of the enemy Powers as far as possible. On the other hand, there was no mention in his letter of any readiness to cede Austrian territory to Italy. Count Czernin, who was well-informed as to essentials in the negotiations but was unacquainted with the text of the Imperial letter, endeavoured in the meanwhile to win over the German Government to the idea of peace. On March 27 an agreement was signed at Vienna between him and Bethmann-Hollweg which provided for a minimum and maximum programme. In the former the restoration of the territorial *status quo ante bellum* of the Central Powers in the East and West was laid down as the condition precedent to their evacuation of the occupied provinces of Russia (except Poland), Serbia, Albania, Greece and Rumania. In the latter, which was to hold good in the event of the war taking a more favourable turn, provision was made for a permanent acquisition of enemy territory in proportion to their respective military achievements. In this event Germany's field of expansion was to be in the East, Austria-Hungary's in Rumania.

Shortly afterwards, on April 3, the Emperor and Czernin arrived at Homburg as guests of the Emperor William. Czernin came forward with a proposal (the connection with Prince Sixtus's *démarche* bring noteworthy) that Germany might make concessions to France in Alsace-Lorraine, and as a substitute for her losses in the West take permanent possession of a Poland supplemented by Galicia. These plans found a basis in the prospect of concluding a favourable peace with Russia, which had opened up shortly before the abdication of the Tsar in March. To reinforce his efforts, Count Czernin, on April 14, sent to the Emperor William a report, drawn up by himself for the Emperor Charles in person, in which the internal situation of the Habsburg Monarchy was painted in the blackest colours, and its collapse, involving a revolution and the downfall of the dynasty, was represented as imminent. At the same time Czernin renewed in authoritative quarters in Germany his offer to compensate the German Empire in case of possible losses in Alsace-Lorraine by the permanent acquisition of Poland enlarged by the addition of Galicia. But the Emperor William and his counsellors refused to open negotiations with the enemy on this basis, and urged the continuation of the war. It soon afterwards became plain that the secret negotiations conducted by Sixtus of Parma with the Entente Powers would not lead to the results desired by the Emperor and Czernin. For Italy held to her bond, and demanded the cession of all those provinces of the Habsburg Monarchy which had been promised her by the Treaty of London. To this, however, the Emperor Charles, particularly in view of the military situation at the time, neither would nor could consent.

The negotiations with the Western Powers having thus for the present led to no tangible results, the Emperor and Czernin decided at Kreuznach (May 17–18) to come to an agreement with the German Government, in which there was no further mention of the cession of Alsace-Lorraine, but in which it was stipulated by Austria-Hungary that not only should her integrity be guaranteed, but she should receive considerable accessions of territory in the Balkans. Germany, furthermore, agreed, in the event of Courland and Lithuania joining and concurrently Poland leaning towards the German Empire, that " Rumania, so far as occupied, with the exception of the Dobruja (frontier anterior to 1913) and a border strip to the south of the Cernavoda-Constanza railway, falls as a separate State into the Austro-Hungarian sphere of interests, subject to a guarantee of Germany's economic interests in Rumania." On the fulfilment of these conditions Austria-Hungary consented to renounce her *condominium* in Poland, and promised to declare her *désinteressement*, political and military, in

Poland. On June 8 the Emperor William and Charles signed an agreement as to Poland's military forces, by which their organization was placed entirely in the hands of Germany.

The war continued. The Quadruple Alliance exerted all its military strength, and even now gained not inconsiderable successes. On the Western front the Germans held at bay the attacks of the French and British troops, lavishly furnished with war material. On the Eastern front the armies of the Alliance fought successfully against the Russians.

In the South the armies of Austria-Hungary, stiffened by German troops, undertook an invasion of Italy, which led to the occupation of further Italian territory. But all these successes did not suffice to compel a desire for peace on the part of the enemy, while, in the countries of the Quadruple Alliance, war weariness, furthered by a skilfully managed propaganda on the part of the Entente, kept spreading to wider circles among the soldiers and citizens of the Central Powers and their allies. This feeling among the people, and the recognition of the fact that the war could only be ended by diplomatic means, decided Czernin to resume with the greatest energy his efforts to achieve a peace which should preserve the vital interests of the Monarchy. In this he was strongly supported by the declaration made by the majority in the German Reichstag on July 19,

1917, in favour of a peace by agreement, in which the forcible acquisition of territory and oppressive political, economic and financial measures were repudiated, and the freedom of the seas and the renunciation by the enemy of the economic blockade of the Central Powers were demanded.

Yet neither the Pope's official efforts for peace nor the secret Revertera-Armand (July-August) and Mensdorff-Smuts (December) negotiations led to tangible results, since the enemy had exact information as to the critical internal situation of the Powers of the Quadruple Alliance, and, counting upon the strong support of the United States for the following year, made conditions to which, in view of her favourable military situation at the end of the year 1917, Germany would not accede. And the attempt of General Smuts to promote the idea of a separate peace with Austria-Hungary on the basis of her being strengthened by a political and economic union with Rumania and Serbia failed, because Czernin refused to leave Germany in the lurch during the war. At this time, moreover, the prospect was opening of concluding a favourable peace in the East which would enable them to fall with their full strength upon their enemies in the West.

The revolution which had taken place in Russia in March, 1917, had not brought peace ; on the contrary, the numerous negotiations which took place between the Central Powers and Russia, having as their aim the conclusion of a separate peace, dragged on inconclusively. The war was waged successfully by Germany, and brought wide territories in the East into the possession of the allies. But a decisive change took place in the attitude of the Russian politicians in November, when the second phase of the Russian revolution—the " social revolutionary " phase led by Kerensky—was succeeded by a third, that of the Bolsheviks, led by Lenin and Trotsky. As early as the end of November the new Government summoned all the belligerents to enter immediately upon an armistice and begin negotiations for the conclusion of a general peace which should assure to every nation freedom of economic and cultural development. When the Entente Powers refused to comply with this summons, the Russians, on December 3, entered into a suspension of hostilities with Germany and her allies, which was to last till December 17. On December 15 the suspension of hostilities was succeeded by an armistice, which was to last till January 14, 1918, and then be continued with the right to denounce it on seven days' notice. Peace negotiations began on December 22 at Brest-Litovsk, and were conducted in public. The upshot was that on December 25 the Quadruple Alliance accepted the Russian proposals for the conclusion of a peace without annexations and indemnities as the basis for a general peace.

At the suggestion of the Russian delegates the negotiations were suspended for ten days, and a request was addressed to the enemies of the Quadruple Alliance that they should take part in further deliberations on the basis of the resolutions adopted on December 25. But the Entente Powers refused. Thereupon negotiations were begun (January 9, 1918) for a separate peace between Russia and the Quadruple Alliance ; but they did not run so smoothly as the majority of Austro-Hungarian politicians had hoped. Trotsky, the chief of the Russian delegation, demanded full freedom for the plebiscites to be held in the Russian provinces occupied by the Central Powers, and with this object proposed that their troops should evacuate them. On the rejection of this proposal by the German and Austro-Hungarian delegates, he protracted the negotiations in order meanwhile to introduce Bolshevik ideas into the territories of the Quadruple Alliance. The progress of the negotiations was hampered by quarrels among the Russians, and by the appearance at Brest-Litovsk of a Ukrainian delegation, which pressed for the establishment of a Russian federal republic. Since on this question no agreement could be arrived at, the representatives of the Ukraine, on January 24, announced the complete independence of the Ukrainian People's Republic, and on February 9 concluded a separate peace with the Quadruple Alliance, which, so far as

8

Austria-Hungary was concerned, left the frontier between the two States unchanged. Inspired by his eagerness to bring to the starving population of Austria, and above all to the inhabitants of Vienna, the longed for " bread peace," which stipulated for the delivery of food-stuffs from the Ukraine, Czernin, in compliance with the ardent desire of the Ukrainian delegation, carried out their demand for the incorporation of the district of Cholm in the newly created republic, and for the erection of East Galicia into an autonomous Austrian Crown territory.

The negotiations with Russia had meanwhile been continued. Czernin, zealously seconded in his efforts for peace by the Emperor Charles, pressed for a conclusion, but met with determined opposition from the German negotiators. On February 10 Trotsky declared that Russia, renouncing a formal treaty of peace, regarded the state of war against the Quadruple Alliance as at an end, and would reduce her troops to a peace footing on all fronts. But since this solution did not meet with the whole-hearted consent of the Central Powers, Germany resumed the struggle. The Austro-Hungarian troops did not enter into the war against Soviet Russia, but after a few days joined the march of the German troops into the Ukraine. The Russians, defeated by Germany in the field, now changed their tactics and declared themselves prepared to conclude a formal peace,

which was signed on March 3 at Brest-Litovsk.
It brought the Habsburg Monarchy no accessions
of territory, but, by the official retirement of the
Russians from the ranks of their enemies, it
involved a considerable strengthening of the
Quadruple Alliance.

Poland had become independent of Russia by
the provisions of the Peace at Brest-Litovsk, but
this did not settle the Polish question. The
negotiations conducted by the Cabinets of Vienna
and Berlin as to the fate of Poland in the spring
and summer of 1917 led to no practical issue,
since the conflicting interests of the two Powers
concerned were shown to be irreconcilable. The
plan advocated by Austria, that the Archduke
Charles Stephen should be made Regent, and afterwards King, was accepted neither by the Emperor
William nor by the German Government. In the
autumn of 1917 the decision made earlier in the
year to abandon Poland to Germany and compensate Austria-Hungary in Rumania was given
up, and the Austro-Polish solution advocated by
the Emperor Charles and Czernin was approved
in principle. In the negotiations which followed
as to the carrying out of this plan, however, the
old antagonism of interests again became apparent.
Germany declared that she would make her
acquiescence in the Austro-Polish solution con-
tingent upon the cession to her of large portions
of Polish territory, as " rectifications of frontier,"

and upon her retaining a decisive influence upon the utilization of the economic and military forces of a Polish State which was not to be incorporated in Austria-Hungary, but merely joined to her by a personal union. To this, however, the Vienna Government would not agree, and once more the attempt to reach a definitive solution of the Polish question broke down.

The Poles, anxious about their future and keenly desirous to make it as favourable as possible to themselves, took advantage of these differences to continue negotiations with both sides, in order to secure for their State the widest possible territorial extension and the greatest possible measure of independence. They resolutely protested against the cession of the district of Cholm to the Ukraine, and on March 4, with the aid of the Poles in the Habsburg Monarchy, they succeeded in obtaining the signature, by the Powers concerned in the conclusion of the Peace Treaty of February 9, of a protocol in which it was laid down that the frontiers between Poland and the Ukraine were to be settled by a new agreement, arrived at with the co-operation of the Poles, and perhaps to be altered in their favour. The negotiations between the Cabinets of Vienna and Berlin as to the future destiny of Poland still went on. The former clung to the Austro-Polish solution, but it was evident from many indications that the German Government showed less and less

inclination to consent to it.   In July, after the
luckless Austrian offensive in Italy, the German
Chancellor, Count Hertling, declared that he would
no longer recognize the Austro-Polish solution.
Poland was to have the free choice of her future
form of government, but before its establishment
must come to arrangements with the Central
Powers permanently calculated to secure their
economic and military interests.   Austria-Hungary
agreed to these proposals in principle.   But the
negotiations which were now entered upon led,
like all the preceding ones, to no definite results,
though they provided the Poles once more with the
desired opportunity for fishing in troubled waters.

The ending of the war between Russia and the
Quadruple Alliance also compelled Rumania to
conclude peace with the victors, having already,
on December 17, 1917, had to submit to an
armistice.   After rather long negotiations the
peace preliminaries were signed at the château of
Buftea, near Bucharest, on March 6, and on May 7
the definite peace ; but the latter was not ratified
by Rumania.   Austria-Hungary received a favourable strategic frontier in the Carpathians, important
economic concessions, and the promise of an
immediate evacuation of the provinces of the
Habsburg Monarchy still occupied by Rumania.
King Ferdinand had to thank the personal
intervention of the Emperor Charles for the fact
that he retained his crown.

The successes in the East, gratifying though they were in themselves, did not deceive the governing circles at the Ballplatz as to the danger on the verge of which they hovered. They knew that the filling up of the seriously depleted ranks of the troops, the production of arms and munitions, the provisioning of the soldiers and of the population, would get more difficult every month. Reports kept coming in as to the increasing war-weariness of the troops and the more and more openly expressed anti-dynastic sentiments of the non-German or non-Magyar portions of the population of the Monarchy, as to the correctness of which there could be no doubt. All these reasons increased the desire of the Emperor and of Czernin to bring the war to an end as quickly as possible. As early as the autumn of 1917 the German Government had been informed from Vienna that Austria-Hungary's strength was exhausted, and she insistently urged sacrifices which might content the enemy. The same point of view had been adhered to during the negotiations at Brest-Litovsk. Germany was to find in the East compensations for the cessions which she must make in the West in order to bring the enemy round the peace table. For the negotiations secretly carried on by several Austro-Hungarian statesmen with the representatives of the Entente States had left no doubt as to the fact that there could be no thought of a serious entry upon peace negotiations on the part of the Western Powers before Germany should have handed in precise declarations which should meet their views on the questions of Belgium and Alsace-Lorraine.

It was thus very opportune for the Court of Vienna when President Wilson, in his Message to Congress of January 8, 1918, defined the Fourteen Points, in which he perceived a suitable basis for the establishment of a lasting peace. It is true that several of these points involved considerable damage to Austro-Hungarian interests ; but in their entirety they seemed to afford Czernin the possibility of initiating peace negotiations. He endeavoured in divers ways, and especially through the mediation of the King of Spain, to enter into negotiations with President Wilson, but in vain. Equally fruitless were the informal conversations carried on by Austro-Hungarian representatives with French delegates in Switzerland and other places. Czernin firmly refused the demand of the Western Powers for the conclusion of a separate peace ; but he continued his efforts at negotiation, though he recognized at the same time that the acceptance of the conditions under which the enemy would be prepared to make peace with the Quadruple Alliance could not be expected from the Germans, above all from the Higher Army Command, since they had already made all preparations for a new campaign in the West which was intended to be decisive.

At the beginning of April, 1918, shortly after this German offensive had successfully begun, Czernin emphasized, in an address to a delegation of the Viennese Town Council, his loyalty to Germany, as proved by his rejection of the French peace offers, which were conditional on the recognition of France's claims to Alsace-Lorraine. Clemenceau declared this assertion to be a lie, and, in the course of the feud that followed, published the letter of the Emperor Charles to Prince Sixtus of March 24, 1917, in which he alluded to his willingness to advocate with his allies France's "just claims" to Alsace-Lorraine. The Austro-Hungarian Monarch's loyalty to his alliance was thus placed in an equivocal light, and Czernin's refusal to accept full responsibility for these proceedings led to his resignation, Count Burian being reappointed as his successor. In order to calm the agitation of the Emperor William and the German statesmen and Generals, the Emperor Charles had to make another "journey to Canossa" at Spa, and there on May 12 he put his signature to agreements for a closer political and military union between the two countries, the coming into force of which would have involved heavy damage to the independence of Austria-Hungary. But since the condition of the validity of this treaty, namely an understanding between the two Powers on the Polish question, broke down, owing to the irreconcilable nature of their divergent interests, the Spa agreement, too, remained a scrap of paper.

Meanwhile Germany was putting forth her last strength in the hope of achieving a decisive success ; but her initial successes were followed by reverses. Austria-Hungary had taken part in the battles on the Western front, but only within modest limits. In June she attempted a sudden attack on Italy with the principal body of her troops. But here, too, the decisive victory which had been expected was not achieved. These failures, together with the ever-increasing lack of effective soldiers, arms, munitions and food-stuffs, deepened the longing of the peoples of the Habsburg Monarchy for peace. In addition, the Emperor Charles became alive to the more and more open opposition of the non-German and non-Magyar peoples of his dominions, and likewise to the revolutionary spirit which was becoming conspicuous among the working classes in many places, and he began to tremble for his crown and the fate of the dynasty. In proportion as the German hope of extorting peace by force of arms diminished, a more favourable prospect seemed to open up for the efforts of Austro-Hungarian statesmen to put an end to the war by way of diplomatic negotiations. At the end of June Baron Kühlmann, the German Secretary of State for Foreign Affairs, had been compelled to resign in consequence of his declaration in the Reichstag that

an end of the war through a purely military decision could not be expected. But by August 14
Ludendorff himself, who had played a prominent
part in bringing about Kühlmann's fall, declared
at Headquarters in Spa that they could no longer
hope to break the military spirit of the foe by
force of arms.

Thus, when Burian again approached the German
Government, he no longer met with any opposition
on principle. Yet great differences presented themselves in the course of the deliberations as to the
method of proceeding to be adopted. The Germans
wanted to wait for an improvement of the military
situation in the West and then begin negotiations
with the enemy through a neutral Power—Holland
or Spain—while Austro-Hungarian statesmen advocated an immediate and open appeal to all the
combatant Powers. At the beginning of September
the new German Foreign Minister, Hintze, spent
some time in Vienna in order to arrive at an agreed
course of action. But since this could not be
achieved, Burian determined, without regard to
Germany's opposition, to have an appeal sent out
to all the belligerents for the opening of peace
negotiations. President Wilson answered, however,
after a few days' interval, that he had repeatedly
and in the plainest terms made known the conditions on which he was prepared to consider the
conclusion of peace ; hence the Government of the
United States could not and would not accept a

proposal for the holding of a conference concerning
a matter in which it had already clearly made
known its attitude and aims.   The Cabinets of
Paris and London were equally cold.   The sole
result of Burian's new effort was the increase of
the Entente's hopes of victory.   On September 15
ensued a violent attack against the Bulgarian Army,
in the ranks of which war-weariness had for long
past made serious inroads.   The Bulgarian troops
offered but little resistance ; great bodies of them
laid down their arms and returned to their homes.
The Sofia Government, at the head of which
Malinov, who was friendly to the Entente, had for
some months taken the place of Radoslavov,
resolved to propose an armistice, which was granted
on September 29 under conditions which signified
for the Central Powers the loss of the Balkans.
King Ferdinand abdicated.   These events, and the
great successes of the English troops in Palestine,
produced their effect upon Turkey.   At the beginning of October the fall of Enver and Talaat took
place at Constantinople, and thus the way was
opened for a separate peace.   An armistice was
concluded between Turkey and the Entente on
October 31, which brought the Dardanelles and the
Bosporus under their power, and pledged the
Turks to break off all relations with the Central
Powers.

Meanwhile the catastrophe had taken place in
Austria-Hungary as well.   Encouraged by the

repeated pronouncements of President Wilson as to the right of nations to self-determination, the separatist ideas of those peoples of the Monarchy which did not acknowledge German or Hungarian nationality became more and more articulate. There were disturbances in various parts, and these disruptive influences made it month by month increasingly difficult to keep the army efficient for war. Both Austria-Hungary and Germany now decided to address to President Wilson the offer of an armistice, to be followed by negotiations for peace. To this offer the President at first made no reply ; and thereupon the Emperor Charles, in order to save the dynasty, issued on October 16 a manifesto in which he proclaimed that Austria, in accordance with the will of her peoples, was to be erected into a Federal State, in which every race would be free to establish its own form of body politic on the territory occupied by it. The union of the Austrian Poles with an independent Polish State was not contemplated. The Imperial manifesto was only to apply to Austria. For Hungary, where they were already working for a personal union and for a complete separation from Austria, the manifesto laid stress upon the integrity of the Hungarian kingdom.

It thus became clear to the Southern Slavs that they must no longer hope for a realization of their national aspirations within the bounds of the Monarchy. But the Emperor's expectation of conciliating the Austrian Slavs by means of the manifesto met with no success. President Wilson, too, rejected the Vienna Cabinet's peace offer. He declared that the Government of the United States had already recognized Czecho-Slovakia as a belligerent Power and the Czecho-Slovak National Council as a belligerent Government, as well as the justice of the national aspirations of the Southern Slavs. It was therefore for these peoples themselves to decide which of the resolutions of the Austrian Government were acceptable to them. Upon this the request for an armistice made by the Emperor Charles at the beginning of October was declared to be no longer in force. During October independent national representative bodies assembled in Prague, Agram, Laibach and Vienna. The Emperor's dominions thus dissolved and slipped from his grasp. These internal movements led to the disintegration of the armies, which up to this moment had fought bravely. The Governments of the several countries constituting the Monarchy, Hungary leading the way, summoned their co-nationals to the defence of their particular frontiers or called them back home. The Emperor tried to save what still could be saved. He was prepared to conclude a separate peace with the enemy on terms which would make possible the continuance of the old Monarchy, even though with diminished territory and as a loose aggregation of separate territorial groups under the dynasty of Habsburg-

Lorraine. On October 24 Count Julius Andrassy —the son of the great Austro-Hungarian statesman—succeeded Burian as Foreign Minister, in order to begin negotiations for a separate peace. Three days later the office of Premier in Austria was given to Heinrich Lammasch, Professor of International Law and a well-known pacifist. On the same day renewed proposals for an armistice were made to President Wilson, and the peace *pourparlers,* which had never been entirely interrupted, were resumed in Switzerland with representatives of the Entente by various spokesmen of the Habsburg Monarchy. Once more, however, they reached no result.

At the end of October, after the revolution in Hungary, and when increasing numbers of the troops fighting in Italy had started homewards, the Austro-Hungarian Army Command asked for an armistice from the Italians, who were victoriously advancing against the demoralized and dissolving Austro-Hungarian forces. This was granted on November 3 on conditions of pitiless severity. Austria-Hungary had to reduce her army at once to a peace footing—only twenty divisions were excepted ; to evacuate all enemy territories still occupied by her troops ; to surrender to the enemy large portions of Austrian territory, and to hand over all war material actually in these territories, as well as the whole of her fleet. By this means all resistance was made impossible even

after the expiry of the armistice. Utterly defence-
less, the Emperor had to place his own fate and
that of the ancient Monarchy in the hands of the
victors. The latter also demanded free passage
for their armies over all roads, railways and water-
ways of the Monarchy. Germany's resistance was
thus to be broken by new dangers threatening her
from the South. It was only under protest, and
bowing to necessity, that the Emperor Charles gave
his consent to these demands, which promised to
be fatal to his ally. The negotiations for a separate
peace were indeed now still carried on by the
diplomatists who remained true to the dynasty, but
they hardly met with a hearing from the Entente
Powers. The process of dissolution ran its course
in the old Monarchy. On November 11 the
Emperor renounced all share in the business of
government in Austria and the Lammasch
Government resigned. The Emperor Charles did
not, however, renounce his crown. On the following day, in the Austrian National Assembly, a
Republic was proclaimed, which was at first
intended to form a component part of the new
German Republic. On November 16 the republican
form of government was introduced in Hungary.
The ancient Austro-Hungarian Monarchy had
thereby ceased to exist ; its rôle as a European
Great Power was at an end.

Thus I return to my starting point, namely, the
interrelation between foreign and internal policies.

I trust that you have gathered from my statements that Austria-Hungary broke down in consequence of the disastrous war. She might, but for the war, have existed as a Great Power for many years longer. The World War was therefore the immediate occasion for the downfall of the old Monarchy. But the deeper causes of its collapse lay in the irreconcilable antagonism of the different nationalities, which aimed at an independence incompatible with the idea of imperial unity and of the ascendancy which the Germans had enjoyed for hundreds of years. Regrets, however, are of no avail. History has pronounced its verdict. Austria-Hungary is no more. But the Austrian problem, as a problem of a free supernational State uniting in an organic and lasting manner the inhabitants of Central and Eastern Europe, is by no means solved by the downfall of the Habsburg Monarchy. It still exists, to be sure, no longer as an Austrian, but as a European problem. The solution of it will be—I feel certain—one of the most difficult but also most important questions of European politics. That a solution may be found not only for the welfare of my own country and of the other nations directly involved, but also for the rescue of Europe's threatened culture, one expression of which I venture to call the new Austrian State, is the hope which I am anxious to express in concluding my lectures.